GREEK
MYTHOLOGY

ΕΚΔΟΣΕΙΣ **ADAM** EDITIONS

© **ADAM EDITIONS**, 32 EPIROU STR., KATO CHALANDRI, 152 31 ATHENS
TEL. 6778440-1, 6774662, FAX. 6774663

www.adam.gr
e-mail: adam.editions@adam.gr

GODS & HEROES · ILIAD · ODYSSEY

GREEK
MYTHOLOGY

MARILENA CARABATEA

INTRODUCTION TO MYTH, ITS TRANSMISSION AND SIGNIFICANCE

Mythology is the science or study of myths. A myth may be a story inspired by either real or imaginary events. Today we use the word myth to refer to legendary tales praising the feats of heroes who wrestle with demons and with real or supernatural forces, and who sacrifice themselves for their country and their ideals. The myths of ancient Greece had a similar content, though their significance was very different and much broader.

The older a civilisation, the likelier it is that myths form an inseparable part of its history and religion. Primitive man invented myths to interpret the 'mysteries' of his daily experience, in order to defend himself and adapt to his environment. As he devised ways to meet the basic requirements for his survival (a place to live and food to eat), he began to attempt to interpret those forces that directly affected his life but which he could not control. His inability to find any logical explanation

for, and his need to understand, all the factors that sometimes made his daily life easier and sometimes more difficult, led him to attribute them to superior powers, which he embodied in the gods and heroes. Human interest in subjects such as the creation of the world, life after death, and natural phenomena is a feature of most ancient civilisations, and is clear from the vast body of myths that have been preserved to the present day. Similarities can often be discerned between the myths

Volute krater by Ergotimos and Kleitias. (c. 570 BC. François Vase, Florence 4209.)

Horseman in the Panathenaic procession in honour of the goddess Athena. (Detail from the south frieze of the Parthenon, c. 447-432 BC. British Museum.)

of different peoples, a circumstance which may be attributed either to the fact that people react in similar ways to similar conditions, whether climatological or political, or to cultural exchanges resulting from the development of trade and travel.

It will be useful to begin by examining the sources from which our knowledge of myths is derived. Greek mythology has been preserved to the present day through the writings of ancient authors and through art. Heroic tales were originally sung by bards in the palaces of the Mycenaean kings (14th-11th c. BC). About the 10th century BC, the Ionians of Asia Minor began to compose longer poems about the lives and achievements of their heroes, thus giving birth to epic poetry. This tradition culminated in the Iliad and the Odyssey, the works of Homer, which date from about the middle of the 8th c. BC.

The question of the creation of the gods and the world attracted the interest of another poet, Hesiod of Boeotia, who was probably a contemporary of Homer. In his

Horseman in the Panathenaic procession in honour of the goddess Athena.
(Detail from the north frieze of the Parthenon, c. 447-432 BC. British Museum.)

poem Theogony, Hesiod sets out the genealogy of the gods and narrates the events that led to the establishing of the power of the twelve Olympian gods; in another poem, entitled Works and Days, he describes the creation of the human race.

Attic art of the Archaic (6th c. BC) and particularly of the Classical (5th c. BC) periods confirms the popularity of the epic tradition. The founders of ancient tragedy, Aeschylus, Sophocles and Euripides, often drew their inspiration from episodes taken from the epic narrative, which they embellished or modified in varying degrees, depending on the requirements of the play. At the same time, the figures of the gods and heroes were predominant in the repertoire of Attic art from as early as the first decades of the 6th c. BC. Vase-painters, sculptors and painters for the most part selected myths that were familiar to their contemporaries. To read the picture adorning a vase, or a piece of sculpture, it is necessary first of all to know the basic elements of the story, and then to decipher the established conventions that identify the individual figures. The most popular figures in myth are normally accompanied by their personal symbols: Zeus, for example, holds the thunderbolt, or Herakles wears the lion's pelt and a quiver full of arrows, and carries a club. In some cases, too, the scenes are ac-companied by inscriptions giving the names of the characters depicted. In the absence of these elements, the modern viewer, at least, is obliged to guess at the identity of some of the figures on the basis of the contextual evidence. Here, ancient observers were at an advantage and probably better able to understand the meaning of a scene, since they had more points of reference.

From the period during which epic poetry evolved, which is known as the Heroic period, myths played an important role in ancient education, and also in the development of ancient Greek society, since they cultivated the belief that the events hymned by Homer and the other epic poets were an account of the glorious past of Greece. Many prose works entitled Genealogies and Histories, which date from the late 6th and 5th c. BC, are attributed to the so-called historiographers. These writers were influenced by the epic tradition and wrote genealogies in their attempt to seek the roots of contemporary history in the heroic past, and thereby demonstrate the continuity of Greek civilisation. Some of them, indeed, rationalised the traditional myths in order to confirm their authenticity. Hekataios of Miletos, for example,

Zeus about to throw the thunderbolt.
(Bronze statuette, 5th c. BC. Athens, National Archaeological Museum.)

(c. 500 BC) states that Kerberos was not the terrifying dog of tradition, which had three heads and vigilantly guarded the gates of Hades, but a snake which was called 'the dog of Hades', since its bite led to death.

Despite this, the first doubts as to the historical value of myth were expressed in antiquity. The first to raise serious objections to the credibility of Hesiod's narrative of the creation of the world were the pre-Socratic philosophers (c. 6th c. BC), who sought to identify the beginnings of things in the natural elements, such as water, air and fire. It was not only philosophical thought, however, that dealt a blow to the authenticity of the myths. In the 5th c. BC, Herodotus, who is known as the 'father of history', makes his position clear, and says that the stories he tells are not myths, but real events which he either experienced himself or heard from eye witnesses. Modern scholarship, however, has demonstrated that some of Herodotus's accounts could better be described as 'legends and traditions' than as historical events.

The first to write history in the modern sense of the word was Thucydides, who describes the events of the Peloponnesian War (431-404 BC) in his Histories. Even Thucydides, however, who was dealing with actual events

Female figure holding a torch and an oinochoe. The torch is regarded as the symbol of Demeter and Persephone, but in the absence of an inscription the figure cannot certainly be identified. (Fragment of a pelike, c. 450-425 BC. Elis, Archaeological Museum.)

and was aware of the nature of the historian's task, does not dispute the historicity of the events narrated in the Homeric poems. Moreover, the case of Troy still occupies modern students. The theory that the epic poems are an expression of the ideals of a heroic age and do not relate to real events, was shaken by the excavations of Heinrich Schliemann, who brought to light the ruins of Troy and Mycenae. The existing evidence, of course, does not confirm that the Achaians really did launch an expedition against

Troy, much less that the cause of the war was the abduction of the 'fair Helen' . The substantiation of some of the elements of myth by the excavation evidence, however, is an indication that the boundaries between myth and history cannot always be drawn with complete certainty.

From the 5th century BC onwards, belief in myths was increasingly shaken. At the end of the century, Plato asserted that in an ideal state myths should be used only as an educational tool to form a person's character, and he accordingly rejects all those myths that in his opinion did not constitute suitable moral precepts. In the 4th c. BC, Aristotle described mythology as a different way of thinking, and stressed that the predominant element in philosophy was reason. Greek mythology nevertheless attracted the interest of many writers in the Hellenistic and Roman periods.

To sum up, it should be stressed that what is today called mythology and deemed a collection of imaginary stories, was one of the corner-stones of ancient Greek civilisation. First, it formed the basis of ancient Greek religion: it was through myths that the gods were established as superior powers who ruled the entire world, imposed order and justice, and determined the fate of every human being. The myths also sang the praises of a glorious past, since they extolled the feats of the heroes and therefore promoted the high ideals of courage, self-sacrifice and patriotism. From the time of Homer until at least the Classical period, the heroes were respected as models, and the prevailing view was that every generation ought to make some significant contribution to the completion of the historical structure, so as to serve as an example for its descendants and honour the civilisation it had inherited. These views and beliefs survived for many centuries. Even in the progressive Athens of the Classical period, in which there were intellectuals like Euripides, who disputed the historicity of the Trojan War, and Thucydides, who wrote 'real history', there was a firmly rooted belief that the Athenians were autochthonous, that is that they were descended from King Kekrops who was born from the soil of Attica.

It might be supposed that in the ancient world myth functioned as a means of interpreting reality. The ancient Greeks used important events as sources of inspiration for the creation of myths; a story based either on reality or on imaginary events, or (as was probably usually the case) on both, was passed from mouth to mouth, gaining credibility and finally establishing itself as important knowledge. It is symptomatic that the majority, if not all, of the Greek cities had a foundation myth; the foundation of most of the cities is an established historical fact, but the authenticity of the myth linked with it cannot be substantiated.

One interesting theory draws a parallel between the first steps of civilisation and the first steps of human beings. Most children in the world grow up with fairy tales and often make up their own imaginary stories; this is probably a method of adapting to reality.

The evolution of civilisation follows a similar course: at first people idealise nature, their past, and their experiences, in order to defend themselves against anything unknown, of which they are afraid. Gradually, however, they acquire greater knowledge and use their reason to account for both natural phenomena and also their personal experiences. As their thinking matures, they distinguish myth from reality, acquire a sense of history, and free themselves of the ghosts of the 'heroic age'.

The Lion Gate on the acropolis at Mycenae. (13th-11th c. BC.)

THE CREATION OF THE WORLD

The oldest complete work on the creation of the world and the establishment of order amongst the society of the gods is the Theogony, by the Boeotian poet Hesiod, which dates from about 700 BC. Creation myths, however, have been preserved in many versions both earlier and later than Hesiod, and reference will briefly be made to the most important features of them.

THE GODS

According to Hesiod, the beginning of creation starts with Chaos, Gaia (Earth) and Eros. Erebos and Night were born from Chaos, while Ouranos and Okeanos sprang from Gaia. The role of Ouranos was at first to cover and therefore to protect Gaia, but he then coupled with her and they became the first gods to rule the world. From their union were born the twelve Titans (Okeanos, Koios, Kreios, Hyperion, Iapetos, Kronos, Theia, Rhea, Themis, Mnemosyne, Phoibe and Tethys), the

**Poseidon, Apollo and Artemis.
(Part of the east frieze of the Parthenon, c. 447-432 BC. Athens, Acropolis Museum.)**

three Kyklopes (Brontes, Steropes and Arges), and, finally, the three hundred-handed giants (Kottos, Gyges and Briares).

Ouranos did not welcome his offspring, however, because he did not want to lose his throne when they grew up, and to prevent this he made his wife hide their children deep in her bowels. Motherly instinct overcame conjugal solidarity, however, and Gaia decided to deploy her female wiles and intelligence in order to free her children. The only way to achieve this aim was to take away her husband's strength and she therefore armed her youngest child, Kronos, with a sickle and arranged a suitable moment for him to cut of his father's genitals. From the seed of Ouranos, which fell into the sea, was born Aphrodite, while from his blood, which was spilt on the earth, were created the Fates, the Giants, and the Meliai Nymphs.

Kronos succeeded his father and took his sister Rhea as his wife; he then freed the rest of his brothers from the bowels of the earth and shared some of his power with them: to Okeanos, who married Tethys, was assigned the task of ruling over the sea and rivers, while Hyperion and Phoibe assumed responsibility for guiding the sun and the stars. The inevitable happened, however, and Kronos was consumed by the same fears that had tormented Ouranos. When Rhea presented him with their first child, he felt his throne threatened, and decided to swallow all his children

Rhea deceives Kronos with a stone wrapped in baby clothes. (Column krater, c. 460 BC. Louvre G 366.)

**Aphrodite, Poseidon, Demeter, Athena, Zeus, Hera, Apollo and Artemis.
(Circular marble altar or base, c. 350-340 BC. Athens, National Archaeological Museum.)**

(Hestia, Demeter, Hera, Hades, Poseidon and Zeus) so that they could never dethrone him. Once again it was the mother who opposed the ambitions of the powerful father. Rhea managed to save her youngest child, Zeus, deceiving her husband with a stone wrapped in swaddling clothes. Kronos swallowed the stone unsuspectingly, and Zeus was brought up on Mount Dikte in Crete in the care of the Nymphs, while the Kouretes danced and clashed their shields to cover the sound of his crying, and Amaltheia, who is described variously as a goat or a Nymph, suckled him with her milk. In time Zeus grew to manhood and became strong enough to dethrone his father and compel him to spew the rest of his children from his entrails.

THE BATTLE OF THE TITANS

ZEUS'S ASCENT to the throne was not universally accepted: Gaia encouraged the Titans, the brothers of Kronos, to revolt and overthrow the new regime.

Zeus and the other members of the Olympic pantheon fortified themselves on Mount Olympos to defend their kingdom. They finally managed to defeat the Titans, but only after winning over the other children of Ouranos and Gaia, the Kyklopes and the hundred-handed giants. Despite the defeat of the Titans, Gaia refused to be reconciled, and next aroused the Giants against the gods of Mount Olympos.

The Battle of the Giants. The Giants are depicted with serpents' legs and human form.
(Detail from the frieze of the Pergamon Altar,
which was dedicated to Zeus. c. 180-150 BC. Berlin, Staatliche Museen.)

THE BATTLE OF THE GIANTS

THE GIANTS are described either as terrible monsters with serpents on their head, a human body and a serpent-tail instead of legs, or as fully armed warriors; in both cases, however, they are regarded as savage beings who do not obey the laws and rules. They attacked the gods on Mount Olympos, throwing stones, trees and firebrands at them, and at the same time upset the order of the world by moving mountains, plunging islands to the depths of the sea, and changing the course of rivers. The gods joined forces in order to confront them; they were final-

**Battle of the Giants.
(Amphora, c. 400-390 BC. Louvre s1667.).**

**Apollo shoots his accurate arrows,
and Artemis menacingly raises
two lighted torches.**

**Poseidon, mounted on horseback
and carrying his trident,
Athena with her spear, and Herakles with
his sword, put their foes to rout.**

ly victorious only when Herakles entered the struggle and Zeus managed to prevent Gaia from getting the magic herb that made the giants invincible.

All these events, which were played out before the Olympic pantheon was finally established, mark periods of great upheaval in the world. The Giants were said to be so powerful that they could moved mountains and change the course of rivers; indeed, according to one version of the Battle of the Giants, Poseidon lifted up an entire island (Nisyros) in order to throw it at his opponents. Since all these episodes are reminiscent of disasters that we now know can be caused by phenomena such as earthquakes, floods, etc., we may assume that stories of this kind give expression to man's need to interpret what is happening in nature. At the same time, however, it has been asserted that the myths dealing with the long conflicts between the gods also have a symbolical significance. The antagonism of Ouranos and Kronos towards their children perhaps alludes to the struggle between the generations, and the inability of the older generation to give place to the younger. The Battle of the Titans and the Battle of the Giants possibly hint at the conflict between two opposed worlds, with the Titans and Giants on the one hand, representing lawless, anarchical societies, and chaos, while the Olympian gods, on the other, are presented as the defenders of natural order and balance. The victory of the gods therefore involves not only the establishment of their power and their worship, but also the triumph of civilisation and order over savagery and anarchy.

Ares, in a chariot driven by Aphrodite, and the two Dioskouroi, on horseback, threaten the Giants with their spears, while Persephone fights with sword in hand.

The twelve gods who established themselves on Mount Olympos ruled the world more democratically than their forefathers. Zeus made himself supreme ruler of the gods and men, but also shared his power with his brothers and sisters, and assigned certain duties to minor deities. Whoever occupied a place amongst the gods was completely responsible for his own actions and decisions. Poseidon could cause a storm or calm the sea for sailors to voyage on, Demeter ensured the fertility of the earth, Apollo gave oracles and taught music, Aphrodite

Zeus threatens the enemy with his thunderbolt, while Nike drives his chariot and Dionysos fights from a chariot drawn by panthers

spread love, Dionysos gave men courage for war, Athena enlightened the world through her wisdom, Hera protected married life and Hephaistos taught the crafts. At the same time, however, Zeus reserved the right to impose order and often intervened with his thunderbolt to resolve major disputes between the immortals; for, as we shall see below, the ancient Greeks gave their gods not only human form, but also human weaknesses. Many myths accordingly refer to the peccadillos and errors of the gods, which, of course, are punished according to the laws of justice and ethics.

This is the picture of the Greek pantheon to be formed from the evidence derived from ancient art and literature. The view that natural phenomena, the maintenance of balance in the world, and human destiny depend on the power and will of the gods demonstrates the human need to comprehend the forces that pull the strings of life. The same reasoning might be used to interpret the weaknesses attributed to the otherwise omnipotent deities. The belief that the immortals who rule the world can feel envy, pain, grief, or love helped people to come to terms with their emotions, which they could not always interpret rationally. Many myths were thus woven around the jealousy and vengeful na-

**Part of the north frieze of the Treasury of the Siphnians at Delphi, c. 530 BC.
Ares and Hermes fight two Giants each.**

**The lions drawing the chariot
of Kybele savage a Giant.**

ture of Hera and the infidelities of Zeus, Demeter mourns
the loss of her daughter, Persephone, like any mother, and
Poseidon does everything he
can to win the heart of Amphitrite and make her his wife.

MANKIND

The gods created human beings and other living creatures from a basic compound of earth and fire, to which they added whatever other materials could be mixed with it. They then gave Prometheus and Epimetheus, the sons of the Titan Iapetos and the Okeanid Klymene, the task of endowing their creations with gifts (Plato, *Protagoras* 320c-322a). The two brothers agreed that Epimetheus should apportion the gifts, and should later call upon Prometheus to oversee his work. Epimetheus called upon all his wisdom to endow all creatures with the appropriate means to ensure their survival and perpetuation; he gave some of them fur, for example, and others wings to fly, and made some of them eaters of grass and others eaters of plants. When it came to man's turn, however, Epimetheus had run out of gifts, and man therefore remained naked and defenceless against nature.

Prometheus felt responsible for his brother's mistake and tried to find some way to help mankind. Since the gifts offered by the gods had been used up, he had to think of something else. Prometheus decided secretly to enter the workshop of Hephaistos and Athena and steal fire. It was a very bold plan, but proved effective: Prometheus not only gave fire to humans, but also taught them how to use it. From this sprang the art of metal-working which made an important contribution to the development of civilisation. Zeus, however, did not want to give mortals the power of fire, and when he saw what had happened, his anger was uncontrollable. He determined to punish Prometheus severely, and ordered him to be taken to the East, and chained to a crag in the Caucasus, where every morning he sent an eagle to devour his liver, which grew whole again during the night (Apollodoros, *Library* 1.7.1). Many years later Herakles freed him from his torment by killing the eagle with his arrows (Aeschylus, *Prometheus Bound* 436-506).

The stories of Epi-

Herakles kills Zeus's eagle with his arrow in order to free Prometheus.
(Krater, c. 610 BC. Athens, National Archaeological Museum 16384.)

metheus and Prometheus complete the cycle of creation myths: the error made by the former and the daring of the latter are an attempt to account for the differences between humans and other living beings. Furthermore, Prometheus was punished in order to restore justice because, whatever his motives, he had violated Zeus's commands and the laws against crimes such as theft and impiety. When Herakles finally put an end to his torment, we may assume that this, too, is at the decision of Zeus who, of course, had not taken pity on Prometheus but probably wanted to give the pan-Hellenic hero yet another opportunity to demonstrate his prowess.

As with most traditions relating to the history of the creation of mankind, the first woman was created after the man in Greek mythology, too, and in this case she was called Pandora, meaning the one who brings gifts. The birth of Pandora was a popular subject in Attic iconography. On a volute krater in Oxford Pandora is depicted from the waist up as she springs from the earth and is welcomed by Epimetheus, while Eros, flying between them, hints at their future relationship, and the scene is watched by Hermes and Zeus. The hammer held by Epimetheus indicates that he is a craftsman, and this specific scene may therefore be inspired by the version of myth according to which woman was created by Epimetheus.

Hesiod (*Works and Days* 42-105) recounts another version of the myth. Hesiod interpreted the unpleasant things that happened in the world as the result of Zeus's vengeance. He represents the omnipotent god as being in competition with weak mortals: Zeus was obliged to cede to mankind the fire that had been stolen by

The Titans Atlas and Prometheus suffer the eternal punishments imposed upon them by Zeus. The former supports the vault of heaven on his shoulders and the latter is chained to a crag in the Caucasus, while every day an eagle devours his liver. (Lakonian kylix, c. 570-560 BC. Vatican, Gregoriano Etrusco Museum 16592.)

Prometheus, but took his revenge by sending woman to them, who was to be the source of all misfortunes. His choice of this version of the myth reveals Hesiod to be a misogynist and a pessimist, since it depicts mankind as being entrapped by the god's anger. A similar pessimism characterises Hesiod's account of the first five races of man (*Works and Days* 109-201), which succeeded each other until they had completed their cycle, when they were covered by the earth.

The idea of the complete destruction of the world is found not only in the writing of Hesiod, but also in myths relating to the terrible floods that wiped out the human race. The most famous of these is the so-called flood of Deukalion (Apollodoros, *Library* 1.7.2-4), the only survivors of which were Deukalion, the son of Prometheus, and his wife Pyrrha, who was the daughter of Epimetheus and Pandora. They survived because they heeded their parents' warnings and built an ark to save themselves. The story to this point is parallel with the story of the flood of Noah in the Old Testament, but naturally the two have different endings. When the flood came to an end,

Deukalion's ark was on the summit of Mount Parnassos, where the two survivors made sacrifices to give thanks to Zeus for their delivery and to pray for the renewal of the human race. The gods heard their prayers and told them to throw stones over their shoulders; from the stones thrown by Deukalion sprang men, and from those thrown by Pyrrha women.

This myth gives expression to the belief that the founders of the most important tribes that dwelt in Greece were descendants of Deukalion and Pyrrha, who were in turn descended from primeval divine forces, since their fathers, Prometheus and Epimetheus, were the children of Titans. This belief reflects the tendency of the ancient Greeks to associate their roots with deities who are supposed to rule the world, in order to justify their superiority and supremacy. The coupling of a god with a mortal woman is, moreover, a motif found very commonly in Greek mythology, since divine origins reinforce the prestige and authority of the heroes.

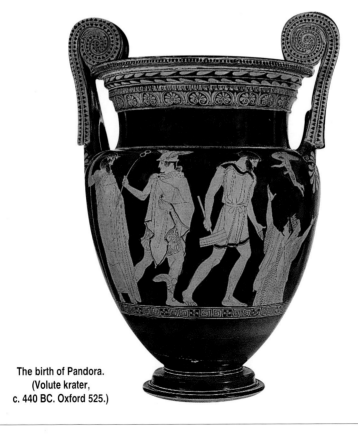

**The birth of Pandora.
(Volute krater,
c. 440 BC. Oxford 525.)**

THE TWELVE OLYMPIAN GODS

ZEUS

ZEUS was the son of Kronos and Rhea; when he grew to manhood he deposed his father and, after hard battles fought against the Titans and Giants, became king of the gods and men. He gathered around him his brothers and sisters and some of his children and created the pantheon of the twelve gods of Olympos. These gods dwelt on the peaks of the mountain and oversaw everything that happened in the world.

The omnipotent god was worshipped in many different forms. The altar to him in the courtyards of houses was normally erected to Zeus Herkeios, who protected the family hearth. Zeus Xenios was the god of hospitality, and all travellers had to be welcomed in his honour. Zeus Polieus was guardian of cities, Zeus Horkios oversaw the observance of oaths, and Zeus Soter was a general protector and benefactor. The oracle of Zeus at Dodona was the oldest in the world and enjoyed fame equal to that of Apollo at Delphi. It attracted large numbers of visitors from many different places and was an important cult centre. The god's priestesses made their prophecies by interpreting the cooing of doves and the rustling of the leaves of a sacred oak tree.

There was also an important cult of Zeus in the famous sanctuary at Olympia. His temple here was dominated by the monumental gold and ivory statue made by the Athenian sculptor Pheidias (437-430 BC). The altar to the god was formed of the ashes of the sacrifices made in his honour, and his priests divined his prophecies by examining the entrails of the sacrificial victims. The sanctuary at Olympia became famous both for its oracle, and because it was there that Herakles founded the Olympic Games in honour of his heavenly father.

Monumental statue of Zeus, who was probably holding a thunderbolt in his right hand. (c. 460 BC. Athens, National Archaeological Museum 15161.)

The eagle was the bird sacred to Zeus, since its wild indomitable nature reflected the power and autocratic character of the god; just as the eagle flies high and sees what is happening on the earth, so Zeus had his eyes fixed untiringly on the world that he ruled.

Zeus took as his queen Hera, one of the daughters of Kronos and Rhea. The fruit of their marriage were Eileithyia, the goddess of childbirth, Ares, the god of war, Hebe, the goddess of youth, and Hephaistos, the god of metallurgy. Zeus also had many offspring from his relationships with other women, both mortal and immortal. He was the father of gods, like Hermes and Dionysos, and several heroes, such as Herakles and Perseus.

The basic characteristic of Zeus was his complete omnipotence. Although he shared his authority with other gods, it was he who imposed order and no deity had the right to dispute his decisions. When Apollo protested about the unjust death of Asklepios, he was punished for his impiety. Similarly, no-one dared to censure Zeus for his infidelities, and even his own wife did not have the power to stop him; she could

Olympian Zeus.
(Silver tetradrachm of Alexander the Great, Dion, Archaeological Museum.)

harm her rivals (such as Leto) or his children (such as Herakles), but not Zeus himself. The king of gods and men had complete control over his actions, and his aim was to impose order in the world and pass on his physical and psychological strength to as many descendants as possible.

The abduction of the young Ganymede by Zeus. Zeus holds his travelling staff and Ganymede a cockerel, a love gift. The god was enchanted by the beauty of the young boy and abducted him to make him winepourer in his palace. (Terracotta group, 475-450 BC. Olympia, Archaeological Museum.)

HERA

HERA was the queen of Mount Olympos: the daughter of Kronos and Rhea, she was chosen by Zeus as his wife, after he established his rule over the world. Their wedding was celebrated with great brilliance and was honoured by all the gods. The wife of the father of gods and men embodied the ideal woman, and was the goddess of marriage and the family who protected lawful wives and their children.

The infidelities of Zeus, however, frequently disturbed her own marriage. Hera continually monitored her husband's movements, and her proverbial jealousy often drove her to extremes.

She herself bore Zeus four children: Eileithyia, the patron goddess of women in childbirth, Ares, the god of War, Hebe, the goddess of youth, who married

Zeus and Hera hold royal sceptres.
(Kylix, c. 430 BC British Museum E 82.)

Herakles and Hephaistos, the god of metallurgy. She drove Hephaistos from Mount Olympos, because she was ashamed of his ugly appearance, and obliged him to live far from the other gods. Hephaistos survived alone by exploiting his innate talent, but he never forgave his mother for her harshness, and as soon as a suitable opportunity presented itself, he took his revenge on her. When he undertook to make two royal thrones for the palace of his parents, he seized the chance to humiliate his mother through an ingenious device: he fixed iron chains to the throne intended for Hera and covered them with elegant decoration, so that they could not be seen. As soon as the goddess sat down the chains wrapped themselves around her body and held her fast.

Head of a statue of Hera from her sanctuary at Argos. (c. 420 BC. Athens, National Archaeological Museum 1571.)

Nobody could set her free from her bonds except Hephaistos himself. Despite the fact that all the other gods tried to persuade him to take pity on his mother, he was intransigent. In the end, Dionysos managed to deceive him by giving him wine to drink and taking him drunk to Mount Olympos. Hephaistos was then compelled to give way, but in return he asked for the beautiful Aphrodite as his wife.

Hera with royal crown and sceptre. (Drawing from a lekythos, c. 470 BC. Basel, Ehel Collection.)

POSEIDON

POSEIDON was the son of Kronos and Rhea; when his brother, Zeus, dethroned their father, he made Poseidon god of the sea and assigned to him rule over the oceans, rivers, lakes and springs.

The symbol of authority of the god of the sea is the trident, just as the sceptre is the symbol of Zeus. Poseidon's trident, however, was also a very powerful weapon; the god used it to attack his enemies, and also to agitate the peaceful sea. Poseidon was renowned for his sharp temper, and both mortals and immortals trembled at his anger. During the Battle of the Giants, he fought courageously against the enemy; so great was his anger that he uprooted a whole island (Nisyros) and threw it at them, thereby turning them to route. Sailors always tried to win his favour to secure a safe voyage; they were well aware that with a single movement of his trident the god could stir up the seas and send travellers to their deaths.

Poseidon's sacred animal was the horse, because he created it and then gave it to mankind.

The Nereid Amphitrite captivated Poseidon with her beauty, and the god decided to win her; the girl yielded to the god's amorous siege and followed him to become queen in his palace, which was in the dark depths of the sea. The fruit of their love was the Triton, a sea god who was a human from the waist upwards and a fish from the waist down.

As we have already seen, Poseidon was one of the most important and powerful gods in ancient

Marble statue of Poseidon from Milos. In his right hand he will have been holding the trident. (c. 150-130 BC. Athens, National Archaeological Museum 235.)

Poseidon abducts Amphitrite, while her sisters, the Nereids, run in confusion and Triton reports the event to the girl's mother, Doris.
(Drawing from a pyxis, c. 460 BC. Athens, National Archaeological Museum 1708.)

Greek mythology. This is confirmed even by the geographical position of Greece: since the social and economic development of the country depended directly upon water, Poseidon's favour must have been of immense value to the success of any commercial or military enterprise, which inevitably involved travel over the sea.

Poseidon and Amphitrite seated on banquet couches.
(Kylix, c. 430 BC. British Museum E 82.)

ATHENA

ATHENA was the daughter of Zeus and the Okeanid Metis, but was born from the head of her omnipotent father. According to the tradition accounting for this myth, when Zeus slept with Metis, he was told that he would have a daughter and a son, and that when the latter grew up he would become more powerful and more intelligent than Zeus himself. The father of the gods decided to swallow his mistress to prevent her giving birth to the male child, who was to threaten his authority and give rise to conflict similar to that of the past. He kept his daughter inside his body, however, and gave birth to her himself. This was a very popular subject in Attic art; on an amphora in the British Museum, the young Athena emerges fully armed from the head of Zeus, who is seated and holds his sceptre; next to the father stands Eileithyia, the goddess of childbirth, who is in fact depicted twice on either side of him, while Hermes and Hephaistos are portrayed at the sides of the scene.

The daughter born from the head of the father of the gods inherited from him the gift of wisdom; she was endowed with discretion, intelligence and resourcefulness and devoted herself to both peace and war. She was adroit and had a restless spirit, and was accordingly honoured as the patron of the crafts, with the epithet (Athena) Ergane. Indeed she worked alongside Hephaistos, the god of metallurgy, and it is said that it was from their joint workshop that Prometheus stole the fire that he gave to human beings.

Athena also inherited from her father his strength and courage, and was ho-

Athena Promachos.
(Panathenaic amphora, 363/2 BC. Athens, National Archaeological Museum.)

noured as the god of war, with the epithet (Athena) Promachos.

The goddess of wisdom, war and the arts was indomitable and completely self-sufficient, and therefore rejected ties of marriage; the epithets (Athena) Parthenos and (Athena) Pallas (which means girl) stressed her purity.

Athena with helmet, aegis, spear and shield, on which is depicted a gorgoneion. (Drawing from an amphora, c. 490 BC. Basel Ka 418.)

The birth of Athena from the head of Zeus. (Amphora, c. 520-510 BC. British Museum B 244.)

APOLLO

APOLLO was the son of Zeus and Leto and the brother of Artemis.

Apollo was the great teacher and patron of the art of music.

Nobody could compete with Apollo playing the lyre or the kithara (a stringed instrument of the same type as the lyre), and those who disputed his talent were harshly punished.

Muses – the nine daughters of Zeus and Mnemosyne (one of the daughters of Ouranos and Gaia), patrons of music, and inspirers of artists; their names are: Kleio, Euterpe, Thaleia, Melpomene, Terpsichore, Erato, Polymnia, Ourania and Kalliope.

Apollo was also famous for his prophetic qualities. Determined to reveal the intentions of his father, Zeus, to mankind, he wandered the length and breadth of Greece, looking for the most suit-

**Leto gives birth to Apollo and Artemis on Delos
with the support of Eileithyia, Athena, Aphrodite and other deities.
(Pyxis, c. 340-330 BC. Athens, National Archaeological Museum 1635.)**

Apollo with his lyre pours a libation from a bowl.
(Kylix,c. 480 BC. Delphi Museum 8410.)

able place to found his oracle. he finally chose Delphi, where he founded his famous pan-Hellenic sanctuary. The fame of the Delphic oracle travelled beyond the borders of the Greek world and every year thousands of visitors consulted the oracle on all kinds of matters, ranging from personal issues to major political decisions. The tripod and the omphalos were the sacred symbols of Apollo and were kept in the inner sanctum of his temple at Delphi. On the Delphic tripod sat the Pythia, the priestess who communicated spiritually with the god and transmitted his prophecies. The omphalos was the sacred stone symbolising the position of Delphi at the centre of the world, for it was here that two eagles released by Zeus met on their way from Mount Olympos to opposite ends of the earth.

The god of music was also skilled in the art of medicine. He taught the secrets of medicine to his son, Asklepios, to whom he gave the gift of relieving people's pain and illness. Apollo was also a highly skilled archer, and often accompanied his sister, Artemis, on her hunting expeditions.

ARTEMIS

ARTEMIS was the sister of Apollo, and the daughter of Zeus and Leto. She was the goddess of the hunt; she had a gift for taming wild animals and catching all kinds of prey (Mistress of the Animals), and at the same time she was patron goddess of nature and young animals. She spent most of her time living free in the forests, engaging in hunting and archery.

Artemis was also regarded as the patron of young women and childbirth. Despite the fact that she herself denied the bonds of marriage, her worship was associated with the marriage ritual. Every bride-to-be dedicated her toys to the goddess, thus leaving the objects associated with her carefree childhood behind her, and assumed the responsibilities of wife; this symbolical act prepared every girl for marriage, the transition from her father's house to the house of her husband. Married women too, however did not neglect the worship of Artemis, because they believed that she protected them during childbirth, and decided on the fate of pregnant women; to propitiate her, they dedicated the chitons of women who had died during childbirth or during confinement, in the sanctuary of the goddess at Brauron in Attica.

Artemis hunts a deer.
(Marble sculpture,
150-100 BC.
Delos Museum A 449.)

DIONYSOS

DIONYSOS was the son of Zeus and the beautiful Semele, daughter of Kadmos and Harmonia; like Athena, however, he was born from his father's body, because his mother died prematurely.

The son of the unfortunate Semele became the god of wine, merry-making and the theatre. He it was who gave men the gift of wine and initiated them into its secrets. Appearing to a virtuous citizen, Ikarios, who lived with his daughter, Erigone, in the deme of Ikaria in Attica (modern Dionysos), he gave him the vine and taught him how to make wine. The delighted Ikarios wished to share the gift of the god with other humans and gave the 'magical liquid' to a group of shepherds; unfortunately, however, he forgot to warn them about its effects; the shepherds, unaware of the symptoms of drunkenness, thought that Ikarios had tried to poison them, and killed him. Erigone died with him, hanging

herself out of her grief. Since that time, wine has been served copiously at banquets and on festive occasions. It should be noted, however, that in the ancient world wine was not drunk 'neat' but was mixed with water in the proportion 1:3 in large open vessels called kraters.

'Orgiastic' rituals were organised in honour of the patron god of merry-making. The god inspired men with Dionysiac frenzy and helped them, through dance and song, to escape from the routine of daily life and their earthly duties. The spirit of the god dominated the souls and mind of his followers, who answered his frenzied call and transcended themselves. From this Dionysiac belief in the transcending of the human 'nature' was born the theatre. Just as Dionysos spiritually dominates his followers, so the actor is dominated by the character he is playing; in both cases man suc-

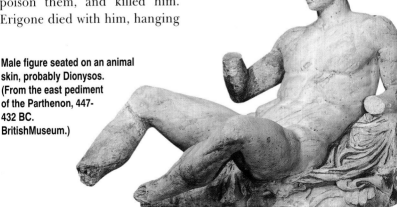

Male figure seated on an animal skin, probably Dionysos. (From the east pediment of the Parthenon, 447-432 BC. BritishMuseum.)

ceeds in leaving behind his own personality and impersonating someone else. The priests of Dionysos were given honorary seats at all Greek theatres in memory of contribution made by the god to the birth of the actor's art.

Dionysos's retinue is called a thiasos (troupe) and consists of satyrs and maenads. Satyrs are monstrous beings, who are men from the waist up and goats from the waist down. The maenads, under the influence of Dionysiac frenzy seek to embody the god himself. Dancing in a state of ecstasy they hunt in the forests and eat their victims raw, believing they can see Dionysos before them.

The god of wild merry-making could not settle in one place and travelled continuously with his followers, spreading his cult to mankind. Dur-

ing his wanderings he encountered many women to whom he was attracted; one of these was Ariadne, the daughter of Minos, whom Theseus abandoned on Naxos in order to satisfy Dionysos's desire.

On a hydria in the British Museum Dionysos lies on a couch and holds a kantharos, with vine-leaves depicted in the background. A satyr entertains him by playing the kithara and another dances to the rhythm of his music, accompanied by a maenad.

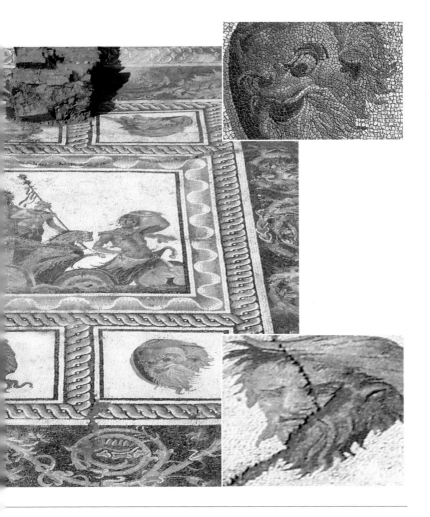

Dionysos crosses the sea on a chariot pulled by two sea-panthers and led by two sea-centaurs. The main scene is flanked by masks of Satyrs and Dionysos. (Mosaic from the so-called 'Villa of Dionysos' at Dion, late 2nd c. AD. Dion.)

DEMETER

DEMETER was the daughter of Kronos and Rhea; when her brother Zeus deposed his father and seized power, he took her with him to Mount Olympos and assigned to her the task of protecting vegetation and farming. On one occasion he slept with her and gave her a beautiful daughter, Persephone.

The cult of Demeter and Persephone was very important in ancient Greece, and its establishment is accounted for by the following myth. One day Kore was playing happily with her friends in the fields, when she was seen by the god of the Underworld, Pluto, who fell in love with her. He immediately rushed up to earth in his chariot and, with the agreement of Zeus, seized her to carry her off to his gloomy kingdom. As she was leaving the light of day behind her forever, Persephone called on her mother for help. It was too late, however, for Hades' chariot had already plunged into the bowels of the earth. Demeter wandered the whole world in her despair, searching for her child, until Helios took pity on her and told her the truth. In her distress,

**Head of the cult statue of Demeter from her temple at Dion.
(320-300 BC. Dion Museum.)**

the goddess continued to wander from place to place until she came to Eleusis. Eleusis was ruled by Keleos, with his wife Metaneira, their four daughters and new-born only son, Demophon. Demeter pretended that she was a simple old woman and persuaded Metaneira to take her on as nurse to her only son. In order to reward the hospitable family, she secretly placed the small Demophon on the fire every night with the intention of making him immortal. One night, however, she was seen by Metaneira, who in her terror began to call out for help. Demeter then revealed her true identity and demanded that the inhabitants of Eleusis build a temple and altar in her honour, so as to atone for their impiety and lack of belief; and so the famous sanctuary at Eleusis was founded. The goddess then shut herself up in her temple and caused a terrible drought on earth, to compel the gods to return her daughter to her. Humans began to die of hunger and thirst, and the need to find some solution became ever more pressing. After Zeus's intervention, Pluto was finally persuaded to be parted from his wife in or-

Demeter, holding a sceptre in her left hand, gives Triptolemos the ears of corn, while Persephone, holding the torches, blesses him.
(Marble relief, c. 440-430 BC. Athens, National Archaeological Museum 126.)

der to save mankind. Before he lost her forever, however, he put a pomegranate into her mouth, knowing that the taste of this earthly fruit would oblige her to return to him. This ruse obliged the gods

Pluto has seized Persephone in his arms and makes off swiftly in his chariot,
while Hermes runs in front and clears the way. The girl attempts to escape reaching her
arms out in despair, with agony etched on her face.
One of her friends looks on in terror and raises her arm to protect herself.
(Wall-painting in the 'tomb of Persephone' at Vergina, middle of the 4th c. BC.)

to find a compromise; it was decided that for one third of the year Persephone would live with her husband, spending the rest of the year with her mother.

The myth of Persephone is an interpretation of the cycle of the seasons, and a symbol of the alternation between life and death. For the four months of the winter, when Kore lives in the Underworld, nature lies dead and fruit is frozen; but when she ascends from the gloom of Hades to keep her mother company on earth, she brings spring with her, and the whole of nature celebrates her arrival and is reborn, to give its fruits. The ascent of Persephone from Hades – the triumph of life over death – was probably celebrated in the famous Eleusinian Mysteries, the secret rituals that took place in the sanctuary of Demeter at Eleusis. The curators of the sanctuary supervised the gradual initiation of believers into the sacred mysteries of the cult of Demeter, but they bound the initiates by a solemn oath never to reveal the rituals. Consequently the rites that took place at the festival are still unknown today; they probably took the form of a ceremony welcoming Persephone to the Upper world, designed to reconcile man to death and give him spiritual tranquillity.

The goddess who was responsible for the rebirth of nature, and her mother, the patron goddess of cereals, taught the benefits of farming to men; the mission was undertaken by Triptolemos, one of their priests at Eleusis.

ARES

ARES was the son of Zeus and Hera; his sisters were Eileithyia, goddess of childbirth, and Hebe, goddess of youth.

Ares was the god of war, forever thirsting for fierce battles and bloody conflicts. He was sharp-tempered and aggressive by nature, in contrast with his half-sister Athena, who was distinguished by her wisdom and sense of strategy (see pp. 34-35).

Despite the fact that Ares was famous for his courage and his handsomeness, he was not very popular with the gods because of his violent, warlike nature.

Ares often created problems; he was the first to be judged by the court of the Areopagos, which was named after him to commemorate this event. This supreme court which only passed judgement on cases of murder, was first constituted when Poseidon accused Ares of violently murdering his son, Halirrhothios. The Areopagos sat in Athens and acquitted the god of war, on the grounds that Halirrhothios had attempted to rape his daughter, Alkippe.

**Ares, the god of war,
with his panoply.
(Volute krater, c. 570 BC. Florence 4209.)**

**The gods watch the Trojan War:
Ares, Aphrodite or Leto,Artemis, Apollo and Zeus.
(Part of the east frieze of the Treasury of the Siphnians at Delphi, c. 530 BC.)**

APHRODITE

WHEN OURANOS was castrated by Kronos, his seed fell into the sea and gave birth to Aphrodite; the goddess emerged from the foaming waves on Cyprus and dazzled the world with her beauty.

Aphrodite was the goddess of love; she planted desire in the souls of mortals and immortals alike and impelled them both to marriage and to adultery. Her wishes were carried out by her faithful acolyte, the winged Eros, who made his victims fall in love with his arrows.

Aphrodite enchanted everyone with her charm. Many of the gods, and also ordinary mortals, attempted to win her, and she often revealed her own choices: she competed with Persephone for the love of the handsome Adonis, and disappointed the goat-footed Pan. She was compelled, however, to marry Hephaistos against her will. This marriage was the price exacted by Hephaistos for freeing his mother, Hera, from the invisible chains of her throne; the god of metallurgy had made a throne-trap to avenge himself on his mother who had rejected him because he was a cripple. In spite of all the gods, Hephaistos desired to marry the beautiful Aphrodite, and it was only when his demand was met that he agreed to free his mother. The goddess of love, however, could

**The Aphrodite of Milos (Venus de Milo).
The goddess of love was the first
respectable woman that artists
dared to depict naked,
because of her matchless beauty.
(Marble statue, 150-125 BC. Louvre.)**

not reconcile herself to a marriage into which she had been compelled to enter. She quickly humiliated her husband by finding consolation in the arms of Ares. From this relationship between the goddess of love, who revitalises humans, and the god of war, who spreads death, was born Harmonia; the union of life and death gave perfection to the world.

Aphrodite bathing.
(Marble statuette, c. 100 BC.
Rhodes, Archaeological Museum.)

Aphrodite accompanied by small figures of winged Eros.
(Kylix, c. 490-480 BC. Berlin, Staatliche Museen F 2291.)

HERMES

HERMES was the son of Zeus and Maia, daughter of the Titan Atlas who supported the vault of heaven on his shoulders. His lively character became evident at a very early age, and he lived free in nature, amusing himself by deceiving the gods and men through his cunning. It is to this spirit of play that the invention of the lyre is owed; Hermes made it from the shell of a tortoise, but later gave it as a reconciliation present to Apollo, the talented god of music, receiving in return the capacity of patron god of shepherds and their flocks.

Hermes was above all, however, the trusty messenger of the gods; he it was who carried their messages and performed a variety of missions.

The messenger of the gods travelled from the higher regions of the heavens down to the deepest depths of the earth, taking not only messages, but also the souls of the dead to the gloom of Hades; Hermes Psychopompos escorted the souls to the gates of the Underworld or handed them over to Charon who took them in his boat to their last residence.

He was also the god of trade and travel, because the missions that he undertook obliged him to be continuously on the move and travel from one end of the earth to the other. Hermes was the patron god of travellers and cared for the security of the roads, which is why the Athenians set up rectangular marble pillars crowned with busts of

The Hermes of Praxiteles. The messenger of the gods holds the young Dionysos on his arm. (Marble statue, c. 330 BC. Olympia, Archaeological Museum.)

Hermes takes Herakles to Mount Olympos.
(Kylix, c. 500 BC. Berlin, Staatliche Museen F 2278.)

Hermes, which were called Hermaic stelai or herms, to mark the most important streets of their city. The god was also worshipped as patron god of the house with the epithet (Hermes) Propylaios, and small marble stelai were erected in front of the doors of houses in his honour. Hermes carried out his missions successfully, winning the trust of gods and the respect of men; at the same time, however, he was patron god of cheats and thieves, because it amused him to play tricks on mortals and immortals alike.

The main symbol of Hermes is the caduceus, a staff that indicated his capacity as bearer of messages and herald of events; in order to move very swiftly he wears a pair of winged boots and a winged hat, the petasos.

Hermes with the caduceus, petasos, winged boots and lyre.
(Drawing from a kalyx krater, c. 480 BC. Basel BS 482.)

HEPHAISTOS

THE ROYAL COUPLE of Zeus and Hera did not love all their children; they threw the new-born Hephaistos out of Olympos, and he was in-

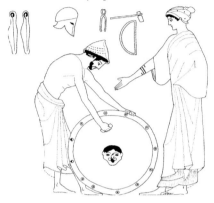

Hephaistos finishes the shield of Achilles, while Thetis waits to receive it. (Drawing from an amphora, c. 490-480 BC. Boston, Museum of Fine Arts 13.188.)

jured as he fell to earth and remained forever lame and a cripple. This rejection of Hephaistos by his parents is accounted for by various versions of the myth: Zeus is said to have punished Hephaistos because he found him plotting with Hera against him, or his mother is said not to have wanted him because she had conceived him against her wishes. According to a third version, however, Hephaistos had a genetic deformity which gave his mother a very difficult delivery. Hera was ashamed of this and sought to hide her shame by driving him away from her.

Hephaistos stood out because of his ugliness amongst the twelve Olympian gods, whose beauty was radiant; in the world of the immortals, he embodied the deformities and imperfections of mor-

Hermes and a satyr take Hephaistos, on horseback, to his mother Hera. (Kalyx krater, c. 490 BC. Louvre G 162.)

tals. However, his physical weaknesses were balanced by his great skill, for he was an excellent craftsman and therefore established himself as the god of metallurgy. He discovered how to melt metals on fire, which he took from the volcanic mountains of Lemnos or from Mount Etna on Sicily, where he had set up his workshop. Athena, the patron goddess of the arts, worked with him, and it was from their joint workshop that Prometheus stole fire to give to mankind.

Hephaistos
(Kylix, c. 430 BC. Berlin, Staatliche Museen F 2537.)

THE LIFE-CYCLE
OF MAN

The twelve Olympian gods ruled the world, along with
many other deities who determined the fate of men.
Amongst them were the forces that pulled the strings of
the daily lives of mortals, from the rising of the sun until
its setting, from birth until death.

THE CALENDAR CYCLE

Many versions been preserved of myths relating to solar and astral phenomena, attesting to the fact that man must have been impressed at a very early date by phenomena such as the succession of days and time in general. In the *Theogony*, Hesiod states that Helios (the sun), Selene (the moon) and Eos (the dawn), were the children of two Titans, Hyperion and Theia. Another version of the myth identifies Helios with Apollo and Selene with Artemis, and interprets the arrows of these gods as symbols of the light they radiate. In art Helios is depicted as a youth, wears his rays as a crown on his head and drives a chariot pulled by winged horses. Every day he travels from one end of the Ocean to the other, starting from the land of the Aithiopes in the East and ending in the land of the Hesperides in the West; on a krater in the British Museum the stars are depicted as young children diving in the Ocean as Helios pursues his

Helios rises in his chariot in the East, while the stars sink in the Ocean. (Kalyx krater, c. 420 BC. British Museum E 466.)

course through the heavens.

When Helios completes his journey Selene bathes in the waters of Ocean, bedecks herself and then ascends into the heavens. She is described as a beautiful young girl who is either mounted on horseback or drives a chariot pulled by winged horses; she is accompanied by a youth, who is none other than Augerinos (the morning and evening star), who brings the stars

Head of Helios.
The holes can be seen by which the metal rays were attached.
(From a marble statue of the god, 220-180 BC. Rhodes, Archaeological Museum.)

and heralds the night.

The following daybreak is brought by Eos, the personification of dawn, accompanied by her son, Eosphoros or Phosphoros. Eosphoros or Phosphoros is identified with the Aposperitis (the evening star) and scholarship has demonstrated that he is also identified with Augerinos, (the morning star) for he is the planet Venus, which is visible only at dawn or in the evening. When nature has been awakened by the arrival of Eos, Helios again sets out on his journey, having returned during the night from the finishing point to the starting point of his course, that is from the West to the East. Ancient poets describe Helios, wearied at the end of the day, lying and relaxing on a golden bed which, during the course of the Moon's reign in heaven, floats on the waters of Ocean and carries him back to the East.

In the Classical period, Greeks believed that Helios and Selene were only worshipped as gods in barbarian religions, and did not therefore honour them as gods, though they paid them equal respect and were in awe of their power. It is significant that in Modern Greek the expression, 'the sun is ruling' means 'the sun is setting', not that he is a king, and 'I have ruled' is used metaphorically to mean 'I have gone

Selene rises on horseback in the heaven.
(Kalyx krater, c. 420 BC. British Museum E 466.)

to sleep'. Another ancient view that has survived to the present day relates to the influence of the phases of the moon on the life of humans. In ancient Greece certain political decisions were taken according to the current phase of the moon. Herodotus (6. 106) tells us that the Spartans never set out to war unless the moon was full. And according to Thucydides (7.50. 3-4), when the Athenians, exhausted by battle and illness, were preparing to withdraw their ships from Syracuse during the Peloponnesian War, there was an eclipse of the moon; the prophets interpreted this as a sign from the gods and advised the Athenians not to move for the following twenty-seven days.

The solar cycle is completed by the days, weeks and seasons, which were also personified in mythology. In the *Odyssey* (XII 129) we learn that Helios had seven sacred herds, each with 350 cattle, tended by two of his daughters in Thrinakia (modern Sicily); no-one was allowed to slaughter these animals, whose number remained always the same and, perhaps not by chance, coincides with the number of days in a solar year. Similarly, the fifty daughters borne by Selene to her great love, Endymion, should probably be identified with the fifty weeks of the year. Finally, in the traditions created after Hesiod's time, the Hours are represented as four or twelve daughters of Helios, and it may therefore be assumed that they were associated with the seasons of the year and the hours of the day.

THE LIFE OF MAN

Convictions relating to the forces that directly influenced the personal life of every individual were dominated by a belief in the power of destiny. In the *Theogony*, the Fates and the Hours are said to be children of Zeus and Themis. On the François vase they are depicted together with the first gods, attending the wedding of Peleus and the Nereid Thetis, praying and offering gifts to the newly-married couple. There were three Fates: Klotho who spins the thread of life, Lachesis who distributes joy and grief and in general determines the course to be taken by the life of every mortal, and Atropos, who cuts the thread of life and brings death. The Hours, of whom there were also three Eirene, Dike and Eunomia have the task of rewarding men for their industry and virtue and are represented in later writings as the protectors of veg-

etation and fertility. The gods oversee all actions of mortals, however, and just as they praise good behaviour, so they also punish injustice. This is the task of the Furies, who were born from the blood of Ouranos that fell on to the earth when he was castrated by Kronos. They are depicted as winged female figures with serpents on their heads and arms, who pursue and torment murderers.

In addition to these three groups of female deities who determine the course of life, and reward and punish, Hesiod mentions many other descendants of the gods who have similar duties; Chaos, who along with Gaia and Eros existed from the beginning of the world, gave birth to Erebos and Night; amongst the children of Night were Nemesis, Hypnos, and Thanatos, Geras, Apate and Iris. The children of Iris were Ponos, Lethe,

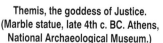

Themis, the goddess of Justice.
(Marble statue, late 4th c. BC. Athens, National Archaeological Museum.)

**Eris, the goddess of strife.
(Drawing from the decoration of a vase, c.
560-550 BC. Berlin,
Staatliche Museen F 1775.)**

Limos, Maches, Phonos, Dysno-
mia and Horkos. And Styx, the
daughter of Okeanos gave to the
world Kratos, Bia, Zelos and Nike.
The personification of abstract
concepts representing social val-
ues (eg. Kratos), personal experiences (eg. Maches) or feelings
(Ponos) in the form of deities
related to the ancient gods of the
Greek pantheon reflects a tendency on the part of mankind
to mythicise those experiences
that impress or inspire awe. Consequently the act of deifying these
concepts consolidates social val-
ues, such as Kratos and Horkos,
propitiates misfortunes, such as
Limos and Mache, and interprets
feelings such as Pothos and Iris.

When the life of man on earth
is over, he is taken to his per-
manent residence in the gloomy
kingdom of Hades, which we shall
now explore.

**Volute krater, c. 570 BC. Florence 4209.
The Hours in the procession of gods attending the wedding of Peleus and Thetis.
The Fates with their mother, Themis, attend the wedding of Peleus and Thetis.**

THE KINGDOM OF THE UNDERWORLD

When Zeus established his authority on Mount Olympos, he assigned rule over the Underworld to Pluto-Hades. The poets describe his kingdom as plunged in the darkness of the bowels of the earth; its gates were vigilantly guarded by Kerberos, a terrible dog with three heads and serpents all over his body, who prevented any soul from ever returning to the world of the living.

The powerful Hades dwelt in the Underworld with his wife, Persephone, the beautiful daughter of Zeus and Demeter (for the abduction of Persephone see pp. 42-44). He is normally represented as a venerable bearded man holding a royal sceptre or a libation vase. He is also identified with Pluto, the god of wealth, whose symbol is a cornucopia. Pluto is said to have been the son of De-

**Hades and Persephone seated on a banquet couch.
(Kylix, c. 440-430 BC. British Museum E 82.)**

**2. Demeter, goddess of agriculture, holds the plough, and Pluto,
the god of prosperity, the cornucopia.
(Pelike, c. 440-430 BC. Athens, National Archaeological Museum 16346.)**

meter and Iasion, and to have been brought up by Eirene; originally he bestowed his gifts only on virtuous mortals, but was blinded by Zeus and obliged to distribute wealth at random. The association of death and wealth in the person of a single god is probably an expression of man's attempt to come to terms with death; the identification of the god who rules men's souls with the god of prosperity relieves the misfortune brought by the former through the happiness distributed by the latter. The painter Polygnotos depicted the kingdom of Hades in the first half of the 5th c. BC in a wall-painting that adorned the Club of the Knidians at Delphi. Although this painting has not survived, we know its content from the detailed description given by the traveller Pausanias in the 2nd c.AD (*Description of Greece* 10.28.2); and the same subject was quite popular in Attic sculpture and vase-painting in the Classical period (5th c.BC). All this evidence allows us to reconstruct the beliefs of the ancient Greeks relating to the journey of souls.

When Atropos decided to cut the thread of a man's life, his soul had to be taken to the kingdom

**Hypnos and Thanatos carry the body of a dead warrior from the battlefield.
(Kylix, c. 500-490 BC. British Museum E 12.)**

of Hades. Some ancient depictions, inspired by epic narratives, portray Hypnos and Thanatos as winged youths removing the body of a dead warrior from the field of battle. The souls of the dead became the charge of Hermes Psychopompos, who either took them to the gates of Hades or delivered them to Charon. Every soul had to have an obol in its mouth to pay the fare for Charon's boat, which transported it to the gates of the Underworld by way of the river Acheron and Lake Acherousia. When the souls arrived at their destination they underwent a trial, which evaluated their actions and decided their fate in the life eternal. The official judges of Hades were Minos, Rhadamanthys and Aiakos, whose lives were distinguished by outstanding honour and wisdom. Those souls who were adjudged honourable drank of the waters of the river Lethe, so as to forget their unpleasant experiences, and were taken to the Elysian Fields, where they found peace and tranquillity. The souls who were found to have been unjust and dishonourable, on the other hand, were handed over to the Furies (Alekto, Tisiphone and Megaira) and taken to Tartaros to suffer condign punishment. Finally, those who had dared to insult the gods were condemned to eternal torment.

A good example of the last is Sisyphos, who was said to have managed to cheat Death twice. On the first occasion he chained Death up, so that no-one died on earth until Ares managed to free him and restore order. On the second occasion, Sisyphos passed through the gates of Hades, but had given his wife instructions to abstain from the customary offerings to the gods of the Underworld; he then used this as a means of persuading Persephone to permit him to go back up to earth, so that the traditional sacrifices would be resumed. He remained there for several more years, since Death did not dare to approach him again. Sisyphos finally died very old and weary, but was severely punished for his double act of impiety: he was condemned to push a large rock up a hill, which rolled back down as soon as he reached the top. On an amphora in the British Museum Sisyphos's torment is watched by Hades, Hermes and Persephone. Another example is Salmoneus who dared to claim that he was Zeus, and therefore was perpetually threatened by a rock hanging over his head; Tityos had once slighted either Hera or Leto and was therefore chained forever while a vulture ate his liver; Ixion was bound to a wheel that turned ceaselessly, because he had attempted to seduce Hera; and Tantalos was tortured by eternal thirst and hunger, because he had dared to test the gods by offering them his own son for dinner.

It may be concluded from these myths that the souls of the honourable were regarded as examples for imitation, while those of the less honourable acted as deterrents. The concept of eternal punishment, however, is probably a reflection of the vanity of life on earth, which consists of a continuous struggle against death and the difficulties ordained by destiny.

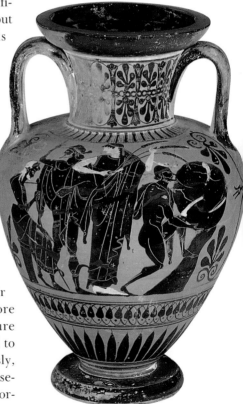

Hades, Hermes and Persephone watch the torment of Sisyphos. (Amphora, c. 510 BC. British Museum B 261.)

HEROES

The feats of the heroes are sung in epic poetry, which
was composed by Homer and other, now unknown,
poets. The heroes were distinguished from ordinary
mortals by their exceptional courage and moral character. They were inferior to the gods, however, because
they were not immortal.

INTRODUCTION

Heroes were mortals who
played leading roles in Greek
mythology. Their personality
was compounded of a variety of
elements. First of all, a mortal's
heroism and strength may be due
to his divine origins, since heroes
were often the offspring of a god
and a mortal; a typical example of
this is furnished by the Dioskouroi
who, as their name shows, were
sons of Zeus. Their mother was
Leda, wife of
Tyndareus,
king of Sparta,
whom Zeus ap-
proached in the
form of a swan.
The founding
fathers of vari-
ous tribes or
the founders of
cities were also
often thought

Herakles kills the Lernaian Hydra.
(Frieze slab, 1st c. AD. Delphi Museum.)

to be the offspring of gods; the
Arkadians, for example, believed
that their founder was Arkas, son
of the Nymph Kallisto and Zeus.
Beliefs of this kind are an expression of the ancient Greek tendency to idealise and mythicise the
past.

Another category includes heroes who were descended from
ancient royal families, who usually
themselves became kings. From
the house of
Pelops, for ex-
ample, who
gave his name
to the Pelopon-
nese, sprang
the Atreidai,
Agamemnon,
king of Myce-
nae, and
Menelaos, who
became king of

Sparta when he married Helen, the daughter of Tyndareus and Leda, mentioned above (the fortunes of these families are bound up with the Trojan War (see pp. 102-127).

It is unfortunately impossible for us today to establish whether the founding fathers, and the members of the royal families that succeeded them, were historical figures. The episodes associated with them may have been inspired by historical events, but they have passed into history by way of myth, for as they were narrated orally, they were embellished with imaginary features emphasising their significance and value. Myths are impressive precisely because they are based on exaggeration, but this means that their historical value for the modern scholar is very limited.

Today the word hero is usually qualified by the adjective brave, and a heroic action is invariably a good deed demanding a high degree of courage. For Homer, heroes were kings and military leaders, and also ordinary warriors, while in modern times they are soldiers who have lost their lives defending their country. The words 'hero' and 'heroine' are applied to the leading actors in ancient Greek literature, and also in modern literature, drama and film, though the meaning of the

The Dioskouroi,
Kastor and Polydeukes,
on horseback, attend their father, Tyndareus,
who is seated holding the royal sceptre.
(Amphora, c. 520-510 BC.
British Museum B 170.)

word is different. The modern 'myth-maker' is inspired by social or historical subjects, which he shapes according to the requirements of a scenario and embellishes with completely imaginary elements; his aim is to entertain, and sometimes to educate the viewer or reader, who is consciously distancing himself from his everyday problems and is transported temporarily into an unreal world.

By contrast, the feats of the heroes in the ancient world, as narrated in epic poetry or tragedy, are presented as historical events that unfolded in a heroic age and were incorporated in reality as part of its past.

HERAKLES

Herakles was a very ancient hero who lived many years before the Trojan War, and his feats are often mentioned in Homer's *Odyssey*. His ancestors were from Argos but he was born at Thebes. His mortal father, Amphitryon, was nephew of Elektryon, who at that time was ruler of Mycenae. During a quarrel Amphitryon accidentally killed his uncle and was obliged to leave the city, with his wife, Alkmene, and flee to Thebes to seek purification. Here Herakles was born. A hero as powerful as he was, however, had to be given divine origins, and it was therefore said that during Amphitryon's absence, Zeus himself lay with Alkmene, assuming the form of her husband.

Zeus's attraction to Alkmene incurred the fatal jealousy of Hera, who decided to destroy the fruit of this love. When Herakles was still an infant she sent two serpents to his cradle to kill him. This episode is depicted on a stamnos in the Louvre Museum: the hero strangles the serpents with his hands, while his brother, Iphikles, flees terrified into the arms of the nurse; next to Herakles stands the goddess Athena, who always protected her favourite hero, and the scene is flanked by Amphitryon and Alkmene who are watching the episode in terror.

Herakles showed that he was no ordinary mortal from a very early age: his divine father had given him special gifts and strength. When he grew up he married Megara, the daughter of Kreon, king of Thebes, and had five children by her. Hera, however, who had still not been revenged, drove the hero mad and in his insanity he killed his wife and children.

Crushed by the terrible crime he had committed, Herakles fled

Herakles, with the lion's pelt and his club, attempts to steal the Delphic tripod. (Amphora, c. 500-490 BC. Wurzburg, Martin von Wagner Museum 500.)

to the Delphic oracle to ask Apollo how he could gain expiation. The god advised him to return to his place of origin and place himself at the service of his cousin, Eurystheus, who was at that time king of Mycenae, Tiryns, and Argos. At Hera's urging, Eurystheus attempted to eliminate the hero by assigning him twelve highly dangerous tasks; these, of course, are the 'twelve labours of Herakles'.

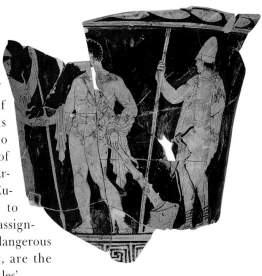

Herakles, accompanied by Iolaos, shakes hands with his patron goddess, Athena. (Fragment of a krater, c. 420-400 BC. Elis, Archaeological Collection.)

The baby Herakles kills the serpents sent by Hera to destroy him. (Stamnos, c. 480 BC. Louvre G 192.)

THE LABOURS OF HERAKLES

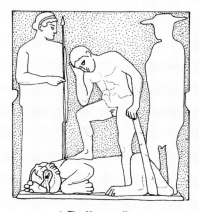

1. The Nemean lion.

2. The Lernaian Hydra.

5. The Keryneian hind.

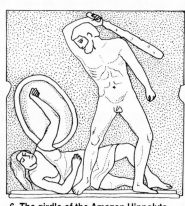

6. The girdle of the Amazon Hippolyta.

9. The cattle of Geryones.

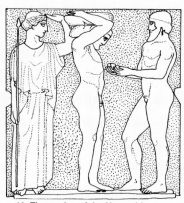

10. The apples of the Hesperides.

The twelve labours of Herakles.
(Metopes from the temple of Zeus at Olympia, c. 470-456 BC.)

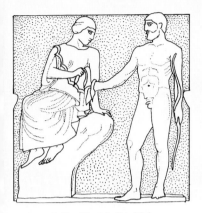

3. The Stymphalian birds.

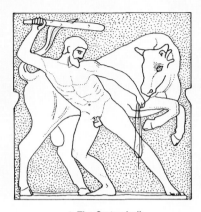

4. The Cretan bull.

7. The Erymanthian boar.

8. The mares of Diomedes.

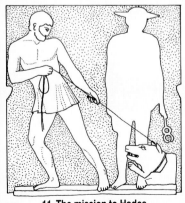

11. The mission to Hades.

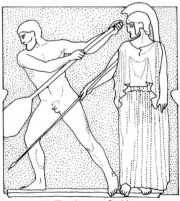

12. The Augean Stables.

Herakles wrestles with the Nemean lion. The scene is watched by Iolaos and Athena.
(Amphora, c. 520 BC. Brescia, Museo Civico.)

1. THE NEMEAN LION

THE INHABITANTS of the region of Nemea were suffering the destructive attacks of a lion, since they had neglected their duties to the gods. The lion was all-powerful and invincible to human weapons, and Herakles was therefore obliged to wrestle with it hand to hand. Here the hero is depicted exhausted after killing the beast, and accompanied by his protectress, Athena, and a male figure (Hermes or Iolaos). The trophy won by Herakles from this victory was the lion's pelt, which the hero wore in almost all depictions of him in Greek art.

2. THE LERNAIAN HYDRA

THE HYDRA was a monster with snakes springing from its body and breathing fire from its mouth that destroyed men, plants and animals. It lived near Lake Lerna in the area of Argos, where it had been sent by Hera to punish Herakles by tormenting the inhabitants of his place of origin. The depiction on a lekythos in the Louvre Museum includes two other elements in the myth: the crab and Iolaos. The crab had emerged from Lake Lerna on the Hydra's orders, in order to help it, and in this scene it bites the hero's foot and hinders his struggles. Iolaos was the faithful companion of Herakles who accompanied him on many of his adventures and made a decisive contribution to this labour: as Herakles cut of the Hydra's heads one by one, Iolaos immediately cauterised the wounds with a torch to prevent them from reduplicating. After his victory, Herakles dipped his arrows in the Hydra's poisonous blood to make them deadly.

**Herakles attempts to kill
the Lernaian Hydra,
while a crab aids the monster
by biting his foot. Iolaos helps him to carry out
this difficult task, and Athena stands by.
(Lekythos, c. 500-490 BC. Louvre CA 598.)**

3. THE STYMPHALIAN BIRDS

HERAKLES was also called upon to rid the northern part of Arkadia from the deadly birds that lived in the thick forest near Lake Stymphalia. Tradition has it that these birds were man-eating and had wings as strong as armour.

4. THE CRETAN BULL

THE NEXT BEAST that the hero had to hunt was a bull that lived in Crete near Knossos, where it created terrible havoc. The presence of the bull on Crete is accounted for by two different myths: it was either the animal used by Zeus to transport

Herakles and Athena, after the killing of the Stymphalian birds.
(Metope from the temple of Zeus at Olympia, c. 470-456 BC.)

Herakles subdues the bull of Knossos.
(Metope from the temple of Zeus at Olympia, c. 470-456 BC.)

his beloved Europa to Crete, or the bull by which Pasiphae, the wife of the Cretan king Minos, bore the Minotaur.

5. THE KERYNEIAN HIND

THIS WAS A HIND dedicated to Artemis with golden horns, which took its name from Mount Keryneia, near Arkadia and Ar-gos, where it lived. Herakles had to catch the animal, which was famous for its fleetness, without wounding it, of course, and bring it alive to Eurystheus. To perform this difficult labour, the hero pursued the hind for many hours, in order to exhaust it, after which he was able to approach it

6. THE GIRDLE OF THE AMAZON HIPPOLYTA

EURYSTHEUS also asked for the elaborate girdle that had been given by Ares to his daughter, the Amazon queen Hippolyta. Herakles gathered together several companions and set out for the city of Themiskyra, on the Black Sea, where the Amazons dwelt. Hera persuaded the Amazons to attack the strangers, but Hippolyta was defeated, while Herakles departed with her girdle.

Herakles and an Amazon.
(Frieze slab, 1st c. AD.
Delphi Museum.)

7. THE ERYMANTHIAN BOAR

A WILD BOAR LIVED on Mount Erymanthos, threatening the inhabitants of Arkadia with destruction. Eurystheus demanded that Herakles should bring this animal alive to Mycenae. To achieve this end, the hero first provoked the animal to chase him and, when it became exhausted after many hours, succeeded in tying it on his shoulders.

8. THE MARES OF DIOMEDES

DIOMEDES, the son of the god Ares, was king of Thrace. He was famous for his terrible mares, which he fed with human flesh; this was a kind of punishment that he inflicted on locals or passers-by if they did not obey him. Eurystheus sent Herakles to rid Thrace of this threat and bring the mares alive to Mycenae. One version of the myth relates that the hero tamed the mares after feeding them on their owner, Diomedes.

9. THE CATTLE OF GERYONES

NO-ONE COULD APPROACH the cattle of the three-bodied Geryones, because they were guarded by Eurytion, son of Ares, and Orthros, a dog with two heads and a serpent's tail. Herakles managed to neutralise the

Herakles delivers the
Erymanthian boar to
Eurystheus, who has hidden in
a jar, terrified.
(Metope from Knossos,
c.450 BC.)

Herakles and the mares of Diomedes.
(Frieze slab, 1st c. AD. Delphi Museum.)

Herakles uses his sword to attack the triple-bodied Geryones.
(Amphora, c. 540 BC. Munich, Staatliche Antikensammlungen.)

guardians of the herd with his club, and thereafter conquered Geryones himself. Many other adventures of Herakles are associated with this labour, for Geryones lived in the far West, at Erytheia, and during the course of his long journey the hero had to deal with many opponents, proving himself the benefactor of many areas that welcomed him as their guest.

10. THE APPLES OF THE HESPERIDES

THE HESPERIDES lived in a sacred garden which was either in the far West or in the North. In the garden were apple trees that produced golden apples from the fruit that Gaia gave Hera as a wedding present. Eurystheus asked Herakles to bring him this sacred fruit, although no-one was allowed to pluck the apples, and Hera had set Ladon, a fearful dragon with a hundred heads, to guard the garden and protect the fruit.

On his way to the garden of the Hesperides, the hero passed by the Caucasus, where Prometheus was bound, and set him free; in return Prometheus told him that his brother, Atlas, would show him the way to the sacred garden. Zeus had sent Atlas to the far West and had made him support the vault of heaven on his shoulders, because Atlas had dared to fight against him in the battle of the Titans.

Herakles met the Titan Atlas in the West and agreed to relieve him temporarily of his burden, so that Atlas could fetch the sacred apples for him. What happens next in the myth is the subject of the metope from the temple of Zeus: Athena helps her protege by supporting his burden with her hand, while Atlas has returned with the golden apples and bargains with Herakles, wishing to take the fruit to Eurystheus himself. Herakles, however, managed to deceive Atlas: pretending to agree to the arrangement, he asked Atlas to support the heaven for one more moment, so that he could put some cushions on his shoulders; Atlas agreed, and Herakles at once seized the apples and made off.

Atlas returns with the apples of the Hesperides,
while Herakles supports the vault of heaven on his shoulders, with the aid of Athena.
(Metope from the temple of Zeus at Olympia, c. 470-456 BC.)

11. THE MISSION TO HADES

EURYSTHEUS was dismayed since, despite the fearful difficulties, Herakles had successfully performed all the labours assigned to him. He therefore decided to assign him a virtually impossible task: the capture of Kerberos who guarded the gates of the Underworld. Kerberos was a sinister dog with three heads and serpents springing from various points of his body. No-one had ever succeeded in eluding this terrible monster and escaping from the gloomy kingdom of Hades. Herakles first terrified Charon with his strength and compelled him to take him to the kingdom of Hades; there he met many souls, and also the king and queen of the Underworld themselves, with whom he discussed his mission. Hades agreed to give Kerberos to him, on condition that he should not use any weapons to capture him.

Herakles drags the bound Kerberos.
(Metope from the temple of Zeus at Olympia, c. 470-456 BC.)

12. THE AUGEAN STABLES

AUGEIAS WAS KING of Elis. His father, Helios, had given him a vast number of flocks and herds; unfortunately, however, the great numbers of animals produced a huge accumulation of dung that threatened the city with pollution and illness. Eurystheus asked Herakles to clean away the dung for Augeias in only a single day. On the metope from the temple of Zeus the hero is depicted shovelling the dung, while the goddess Athena supervises the task. The hero completed this labour very quickly by digging ditches around the fields and collecting the dung in them, after which he diverted the course of two nearby rivers, the Alpheios and the Peneios, which flowed down the ditches and carried away the dung in their streams.

Herakles cleans the Augean stables.
(Metope from the temple of Zeus at Olympia, c. 470-456 BC.)

THE REST OF HERAKLES' LIFE

fter Herakles had completed his service with Eurystheus, he decided to start a new life. When Herakles went down to Hades to fetch Kerberos, he had met Meleager, who asked him to go to Kalydon and ask his father, king Oineus, for the hand of his sister, Deianeira. When he arrived in Kalydon, Herakles found that he had been preceded by the river god Acheloos, who was insisting on marrying Deianeira against her will. Urged on by the bride herself, the hero wrestled with the river god and defeated him, thus successfully fulfilling the promise he had given to the soul of Meleager. After the wedding ceremony the newly married couple set off for Tiryns. On their way they had to cross the river Euenos, where the Centaur Nessos lived; like all the other Centaurs, he had the form of a man from the waist up and a horse from the waist down. Nessos took Deianeira in

Oineus watches Herakles attack the Centaur Nessos to save his wife, Deianeira.
(Stamnos, c. 450-440 BC. British Museum 1896.7-16.5)

Herakles and Deianeira, with Hyllos in her arms, together with Athena and Oineus.
(Pelike, c. 480-470 BC Louvre G 229.)

his arms on the pretext that the gods had assigned to him the task of carrying travellers from one bank of the river to the other; but half way across he began to make love to her and the woman screamed to warn her husband. Herakles then fired one of his arrows, tipped with the poisonous blood of the Lernaian Hydra, and fatally wounded the Centaur. Nessos made sure he had his revenge, howev-er. Just before he died he told Deianeira that his blood had aphrodisiac properties and urged her to gather it, as it ran from his wound, and keep it away from the light of the sun.

For several years Herakles and Deianeira, together with their son Hyllos, lived happily at Tiryns. On a pelike in the Louvre, the hero is depicted as a family head: although he is holding the lion's pelt, bow and club, he is not naked as usual, but wears a himation; Hyllos, in his mother's arms, reaches out his hands to touch his father, and the happy family is flanked by Oineus and Athena. The event that marked the beginning of the end of Herakles' family bliss was his decision to take part in an archery contest organised by Eurytos, king of Oichalia (the precise location of which has not been established), the prize for the victor being his daughter, Iole. As was to be expected, the hero excelled in the competition, but the king refused to honour his promise, because the victor was already married and therefore could not take Iole as his lawful wife. In his anger, Herakles stole the horses of Eurytos and returned to Tiryns. Shortly afterwards, he was visited there by Iphitos who demanded his father's horses; Herakles killed him, however. Once again the hero had to flee his country in order to seek expiation. When he came to the Delphic oracle to consult Apollo, the Pythia refused to answer him, because he bore the pollution of a murder committed in violation of the rules of hospitality. The Pythia's answer enraged Herakles even more, and he snatched the sacred tripod of Apollo from the sanctuary with the aim of founding his own oracle at Pheneos.

This was the cause of the fearful con-

The struggle between Herakles and Apollo for the Delphic tripod.
(East pediment of the Treasury of the Siphnians at Delphi, c. 530 BC.)

flict that broke out between Apollo and Herakles, which was resolved only after Zeus intervened and threw a thunderbolt between them. In the end, Herakles and his family fled to Trachis, where he was the guest of king Keyx.

Trachis is the setting of Sophocles' tragedy the *Trachinian Women*, which is the first full narrative of the events leading to Herakles' death. The tragedy begins with Deianeira announcing that her husband has been away for three years and three months, and noting that the Delphic oracle had predicted that after this period Herakles would either die or would be redeemed.

Alarmed, she sends her son, Hyllos, to look for his father. She soon learns from a messenger that her husband had received instructions from Zeus to serve queen Omphale (probably in Lydia) in order to expiate the murder of Iphitos. After this he had conquered and destroyed Oichalia and had taken Iole as his servant, and had already sent her to Trachis. Although the messenger does not reveal to Deianeira that Herakles' expedition against Oichalia had amorous motives, she quickly learns the truth, and decides to use the love potion given to her by the Centaur Nessos before he died, so that she could again win the love of her husband. She chooses an elegant cloak and smears it with the magical fluid, before

handing it to the messenger, with instructions to give it to Herakles himself and to keep it away from the light of the sun until her husband put it on. The queen realises her tragic mistake after the messenger has already departed: the gift of a man who had fallen victim to her husband's strength could bode no good. Meanwhile, Herakles delightedly puts on his wife's present, but the garment immediately clings to his skin and causes him terrible pain. Hyllos returns to Trachis, tells his mother what has happened and blames her for it. Deianeira then leaves the palace and puts an end to her own life, where-upon Hyllos learns his mother's real intentions and realises that he has accused her unjustly. He then tells his father, who realises that he has come to the end of his life; he asks Hyllos to take him to the top of Mount Oite and burn his body on a large pyre to free him from the pain. Hyllos, overwhelmed with grief, is persuaded to carry out his father's instructions, but at the last minute cannot bring himself to set fire to the pyre; the hero Philoktetes then appears, and is persuaded to contribute to the redeeming of the hero, in return for which Herakles gives him his bow and arrows. The end of the myth is known

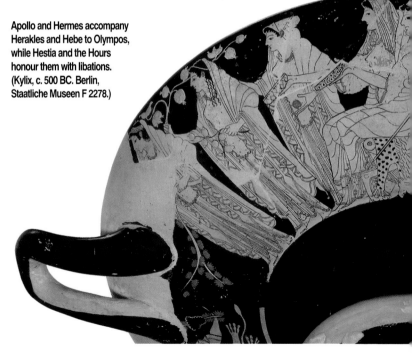

Apollo and Hermes accompany Herakles and Hebe to Olympos, while Hestia and the Hours honour them with libations. (Kylix, c. 500 BC. Berlin, Staatliche Museen F 2278.)

from other sources: the goddess Athena descends in her chariot, raises Herakles from the pyre and takes him with her to Mount Olympos, where he is welcomed by the gods. Herakles is rewarded for his feats by a place amongst the twelve gods of Olympos, becomes immortal, and marries Hebe (the goddess of youth) who gives him the gift of eternal youth. The wedding of Herakles and Hebe is depicted on a kylix in the Berlin Museum: the couple are led by Apollo and Hermes, while Hestia and the Hours pour libations in their honour; on the other side of the vase, which is preserved in fragments, are depicted Zeus and Hera, Poseidon and Amphitrite, Ares and Aphrodite, Dionysos and Ariadne, and Iris.

Eurystheus continued to persecute Herakles' house, however: he banned his descendants from the Argolid and forbade them to enter Boeotia. In Euripides' tragedy *The Herakleidai*, the children of Herakles seek protection from Theseus in Athens, as a result of which the Argives marched against Attica; the Athenians and the Herakleidai routed their opponents and Hyllos killed the fiend Eurystheus. The positive outcome of the battle opened the way for the return of the Herakleidai to the Peloponnese, but the Delphic oracle predicted that it was only the third generation of descendants of the pan-Hellenic hero that would rule in his place of origin; for the next sixty years, therefore, the Argolid was ruled by the family of Atreus, the brother of Eurystheus's wife, until it was exterminated after the Trojan War.

ATTIC MYTHS AND THESEUS

THE ORIGINS OF THE ATHENIANS
AND THEIR EARLIEST KINGS

The traditional accounts of the foundation of Athens state that the Athenians were descended from Kekrops, who was an offspring of the Attic soil. This belief was frequently sung by Attic authors and artists, who took every opportunity to stress proudly that the Athenians differed from the rest of the Greeks in being indigenous. In art the origins of Kekrops are indicated in the manner he is depicted, with the form of a man from the waist up and of a serpent from the waist down; his association with a chthonic being like the serpent, which is in continual contact with the earth, is a clear allusion to his origins. Kekrops was the earliest king of Athens and had a wife Aglauros, who bore him four children: Erysichthon, Aglauros, Herse and Pandrosos. Kekrops is said to have instituted marriage and burial and to have organised all the independent demes of Attica into a kind of federal state. During his

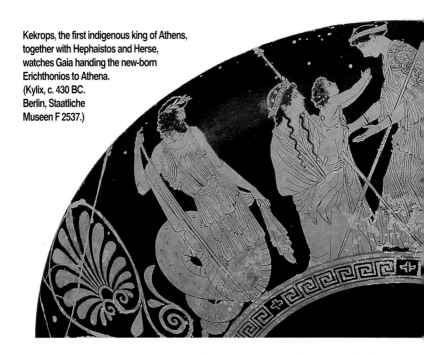

Kekrops, the first indigenous king of Athens, together with Hephaistos and Herse, watches Gaia handing the new-born Erichthonios to Athena.
(Kylix, c. 430 BC.
Berlin, Staatliche
Museen F 2537.)

reign, Athena and Poseidon competed for the title of official patron of the city. The contest was judged on the basis of the gifts offered by the two gods, and the decision was taken either by Kekrops alone or by a council of gods in which the king himself naturally took part. This episode is depicted on a hydria in the Hermitage Museum: the olive tree that grew when Athena struck the rock of the Acropolis with her spear is depicted between the two rivals; at the right Poseidon holds the reigns of a horse in one hand and with the other raises his trident in order to strike the rock and cause the spring to gush forth. The snake, which slithers at the feet of the gods, probably symbolised the

chthonic origins of the Athenians, and the small figure of Nike flying between them holds her arms towards Athena as though pronouncing the outcome of the contest. In the end Athena's gift was preferred over the offering from Poseidon, because the olive was an omen of peace and prosperity for the city, unlike water which was to be found in abundance around the Attic peninsula, and the horse which was regarded as an animal of war. Since that time Athena has continued to act as patron and benefactor of her city. In a scene on a skyphos in the Louvre Museum the goddess contributes to the building of the walls of Athens by leading a Giant who is carrying a huge rock. Athena is also connected with Erichthonios, one of the earliest kings of the city. Erichthonios is said to have been born from the seed of Hephaistos that fell on the earth when the virgin Athena rejected his amorous advances. On a

**Athena competes with Poseidon for the official patronage of the city of Athens.
(Drawing from the decoration of a hydria, c.400-350 BC. Hermitage Museum KAB 6a.)**

kylix in Berlin, Gaia hands the new-born infant to Athena; the figure at the left with the serpent's body is, of course, Kekrops, and the scene is completed at the right by Hephaistos and Herse, a reference to the ending of this myth. Athena loved Erichthonios and brought him up as though he were her actual child; at one point she put him in a box with two snakes for his protection, and entrusted the box to the daughters of Kekrops with instructions always to keep it closed. Overcome by their curiosity, however, they opened it, were driven insane by what they saw, and jumped from the Acropolis rock.

When Erichthonios ascended to the throne of Athens he paid special honour to Athena who had brought him up; he devoted a xoanon (a wooden statue) of her on the Acropolis and, according to the myth, it was he who established the festival of the Panathenaia in her honour. Erichthonios was succeeded by his son, Pandion, and he in turn by his son, Erechtheus. His descendants, the Erectheids, ruled Athens for several generations, after which the throne passed to the children of Theseus, the Theseids. The recurrence of the compound *chthon*, meaning earth, in the name of some of the kings

(Erysichthon, Erichthonios, and Erechtheus) is an allusion to their indigenous origins. This list of the successive kings, of course, has no historical value for modern research, but the authority enjoyed by these myths in antiquity should not be underestimated; they formed the connecting link between the historical period and the glorious past of Athens, and consolidated the view that the Athenians were derived from their indigenous kings, and were thus born and bred on Attic soil.

INTERPRETATION

Beginning in the 6th century BC, Athens gradually developed into an important power in the Greek world. In 594-593 BC Solon became archon and passed his legislation. At the end of the 6th century, the tyranny of Peisistratos was abolished. In 508-507 BC, the archon Kleisthenes organised the inhabitants of Attica into ten tribes. Athens made an important contribution to checking the Persian forces, who were defeated at the battle of Marathon (490 BC) and the naval battle of Salamis (480 BC). To protect the Greek cities from the Persian threat, the Athenians organised the Delian Confederacy, which established Athens as a powerful force in Greece. The history of the city was directly linked with its

mythical past. The reforms of Kleisthenes (508-507 BC) were sealed by the Delphic oracle, which chose ten Attic heroes to give their names to the ten tribes. Furthermore, one tradition has it that two of the major Greek peoples were descended from Athenians; Xouthos, the son of Hellen, fled from Thessaly to Attica. There he married Kreousa, the daughter of king Erechtheus, and had two sons, Ion and Achaios, who became the founding fathers of the Ionians and the Achaians

An excellent example of the influence enjoyed by myths in historical Athens is provided by Euripides' tragedy *Ion* (413 BC), in which the poet claims that Apollo was the real father of Ion. Thus, at the very period that the Athenians were trying to retain their influence over Ionia, the tradition was created that the founding father of the Ionians was the son of a god and an indigenous Athenian woman: this can hardly have been mere coincidence.

The greater the power of Athens grew, the more the links with her mythical past were stressed. The message that the city had taken and continued to take the lead was strongly expressed in the art and literature of Classical Athens. The talents and feats of Theseus, the supreme Athenian hero and king. rival the multi-faceted personality of the pan-Hellenic hero Herakles.

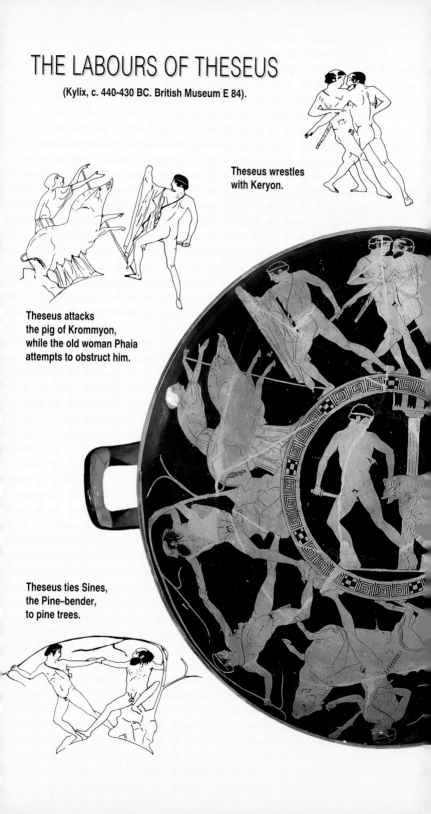

THE LABOURS OF THESEUS

(Kylix, c. 440-430 BC. British Museum E 84).

Theseus wrestles
with Keryon.

Theseus attacks
the pig of Krommyon,
while the old woman Phaia
attempts to obstruct him.

Theseus ties Sines,
the Pine–bender,
to pine trees.

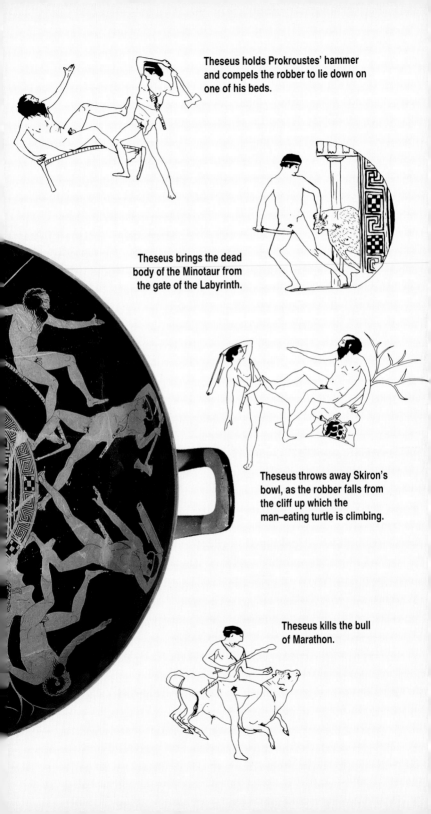

Theseus holds Prokroustes' hammer and compels the robber to lie down on one of his beds.

Theseus brings the dead body of the Minotaur from the gate of the Labyrinth.

Theseus throws away Skiron's bowl, as the robber falls from the cliff up which the man-eating turtle is climbing.

Theseus kills the bull of Marathon.

THESEUS

THE BIRTH OF THESEUS

WHEN AIGEUS became king of Athens, he visited the Delphic oracle to learn the reason why he had not yet acquired any successors. The Pythia, as always, gave him an enigmatic reply: 'Do not open the mouth of the wine-flask until you reach Athens.' Aigeus was unable to interpret the oracle, and therefore decided, before returning to Athens, to go to Troizen to consult king Pittheus, who was famous for his wisdom. Pittheus understood the meaning of Pythia's words and decided to exploit the situation to strengthen the links between Troizen and Athens. He is said to have convinced Aigeus, either by making him drunk, or through persuasion, to spend the night with his daughter, Aithra, who in the end brought him the successor he desired. Before he departed,

Theseus lifts the rock and finds his father's sword and sandals.
Aithra watches her son proudly.
(Clay tablet, 1st c. AD. British Museum D 594.)

Aigeus concealed his sandals and sword beneath a rock and told Aithra that if she bore a son she was to reveal the hiding place to him when he grew up. If he had the strength to raise the rock on his own, she was to send him to Athens with the sandals and sword, so that Aigeus would be able to recognise him. Aigeus then returned to Athens and Aithra bore Theseus nine months later. It was not enough, however, for a hero of this stature to be the offspring of royal families; his bravery transcended human bounds, and therefore tradition tells us that Aithra had coupled with Poseidon before she lay with Aigeus, and the god of the sea was therefore recognised as the hero's heavenly father. When Theseus grew to manhood, he raised the rock and found the things concealed there by his father, took them, and set out on his journey to meet him.

THE LABOURS OF THESEUS

ON HIS WAY from Troizen to Athens, the young Theseus encountered robbers and evil-doers who were threatening the safety of travellers, wrestled with them, and finally killed them using their own weapons. First, as he crossed from Epidauros, he met Periphetes, who killed passers-by with an iron club; Theseus, destroyed the villain and kept his club. At Kenchreai (a harbour of Corinth) lurked Sines,

Theseus and Ariadne.
(Oinochoe, 7th c. BC. Herakleion Museum.)

called the Pine-bender, because he used to tie passers-by to two trees that he bent over, which he then released so that they tore their bodies apart. At Krommyon lived a pig that caused great destruction; the animal was protected by an old woman called Phaia, who tried to persuade the hero to take pity on it, but he attacked it with stones and ultimately managed to kill it with his sword. When Theseus came to the Skironian Rocks (modern Kakia Skala) he found himself face to face with the robber Skiron, who compelled his victims to wash his feet and, as they stooped, pushed them off the rock so that they fell into the sea, where they were devoured by a turtle; the hero killed Skiron in the same way. After this Theseus won a wrestling match with Kerkyon, who killed passers-by on the way from Eleusis, compelling them to wrestle with him. Finally, at some point of the Sacred Way, which linked Eleusis with Athens, there lived Prokroustes; he made passers-by lie down on a bed which was either too long or too short, depending on their height. He then killed them all by stretching the bodies of the short ones until they were long enough for the bed, and cutting off the extremities of the tall ones that stuck out from it. Prokroustes met the same fate as his victims, and after all these adventures, Theseus came victorious to Athens. This event is represent-

ed in the scene on an amphora in the British Museum, in which Aigeus shakes the hand of his son, while Aithra bids him farewell and his heavenly father, Poseidon, looks on. As we have seen already, these labours of Theseus took place during his journey from Troizen to Athens, and they therefore probably symbolise the transition of the hero from his childhood, which he passed at Troizen, to the mature phase of his life, which is associated with Athens, of which he later became king. On a metope of the Treasury of the Siphnians at Delphi, Theseus is presented, triumphant, to the goddess Athena, who welcomes him to her city. Nevertheless, Theseus had to undergo other trials before he was ultimately

Poseidon watches Aithra bidding farewell to Theseus and Aigeus welcoming him.
(Amphora, c. 470-460 BC. British Museum E 264.)

Athena welcomes Theseus to her city.
(Metope of the Treasury of the Athenians at Delphi, c. 530-500 BC).

recognised by his father. When the hero arrived at Athens, Aigeus had married Medea, a demoniacal woman who had killed her own children out of jealousy of her previous husband, Jason. She immediately recognised Theseus, even before Aigeus had realised that the stranger who had come to the city was really his son. Realising that his arrival would affect their marriage, she devised a plan to eliminate him: she persuaded Aigeus to test the 'stranger' by asking him to kill the terrible bull that was wreaking havoc at Marathon. The hero, however, did not succumb to this opponent, either, but managed to kill the fearsome animal and spare Marathon from the destruction it was causing. Medea was disappointed at the failure of her design, but did not give up; she at once prepared a poison, which she intended to offer to their guest during the banquet to be given in his honour. At the last moment, however, Theseus produced his father's symbols (the sword and sandals) and Aigeus recognised him, welcomed his son

**Theseus wrestles with the Minotaur.
(Vase, 6th c. BC. Herakleion Museum.)**

kind of tax, which Athens was obliged to pay every nine years to Minos, the king of Crete, to appease him for the death of his son, who had been killed in Attica. Theseus decided to go to Crete himself in order to free his city from this terrible obligation. The ship with the young men and women set out from Athens with black sails. It had been agreed that if the mission was successful and the young people were saved, the ship should return with white sails hanging from its masts. An important contribution to their success was made by the daughter of Minos, Ariadne, who was captivated by Theseus and decided to help him. The Minotaur was shut up in the labyrinth, a vast area with many corridors and passages, in which anyone who entered got lost, because it was impossible to find the exit. Theseus overcame this obstacle with the help of Ariadne, who gave him a ball of thread, having first tied the end of the thread to the entrance to the labyrinth. As the hero penetrated deep into the labyrinth, he gradually unwound the ball of wool, and having successfully killed the Minotaur, he had only to rewind the ball in order to return to the light of day.

The triumphant Athenians boarded their ship and set off on the return journey. With them went Ariadne, because Theseus had promised that he would make her

joyfully to the palace, and punished his cunning wife with exile. Finally Theseus was proclaimed the rightful successor of his father to the throne of Athens. His problems were not yet over, however; that year the Athenians had to send seven young men and seven girls to Crete to be given as food to the Minotaur. The Minotaur was a monster with the head of a bull and the body of a man, who had been born from the union of Pasiphae, the queen of Crete, and the bull sent by Poseidon to the island (possibly the same animal brought by Herakles to Mycenae, which Theseus had killed at Marathon). The sacrifice of the fourteen Athenian youths was a

Theseus abducts the Amazon Antiope.
(Pediment from the temple of Apollo at Eretria, c. 510 BC. Eretria Museum.)

his wife. During the voyage they stopped at the island of Naxos, where the beautiful Ariadne attracted the attention of the god Dionysos; then Athena intervened and advised the hero to leave his beloved on the island, because, of course, it would not be sensible to oppose the desires of a god. The Athenians also put in at Delos, where they offered sacrifices to Apollo and, clasping each other's hands danced the *geranos*, a dance whose movements mimic their wanderings inside the labyrinth. This episode is depicted on the neck of the François vase in Florence, on which the young Athenian men and women are dancing their way onto their ship. Unhappily, however, because of their enthusiasm and the festivities, they forgot to raise the white sails. When Aigeus saw the ship returning from afar with black sails, he believed that his son had died and in his despair threw himself off the rock on which he stood and was killed. Since that time the sea which re-

ceived the unhappy father has been called the Aegean Sea.

Theseus was distressed when he was told about the pointless death of his father, but soon had to assume his duties. Having been officially proclaimed king of the city, he married Phaidra, who gave him two sons, Akamas and Demophon. His most important task, while he was ruler of Athens, was the unification of all the settlements of Attica into one 'state' with a single government, and the establishment of the festival of the *Synoikia,* ('Unification') in commemoration of this event. He also defeated the army of Amazons that appeared outside his city; and he fought on the side of his close friend Peirithoos, king of the Lapiths in Thessaly, when the Centaurs invaded his wedding feast.

The hero's death is associated with a story that probably took place when his wife was no longer alive. Theseus and Peirithoos decided that, because of their courage and their origins, they ought to

marry women worthy of them. Theseus desired the 'fair Helen', and with the assistance of his friend he carried her off from the palace of her father, Tyndareus, at Sparta. Helen's brothers, the Dioskouroi, who were also very strong because they were the children of Zeus, managed to rescue her, however, and took revenge on Theseus by compelling his mother, Aithra, to enter their sister's service. Aithra followed Helen to Troy as her servant, where she was to be saved by her grandchildren, Akamas and Demophon.

Peirithoos was even bolder, and wanted to win Persephone, the wife of Hades, and the two heroes were therefore obliged to go down to the Underworld. Hades, however, who was aware of their intentions, deceived them; he pretended to make them welcome and offered them two luxurious thrones to sit on. The heroes accepted his hospitality, but the god pinned them forever to these seats and thus punished them for their impiety. According to one view, Theseus never returned from Hades and died in this way. Other myths say that when Herakles descended to the Underworld in order to capture Kerberos, he met the two heroes, but succeeded in freeing only Theseus, who when he returned to Athens found Menestheus on the throne and was obliged to leave the city. Finally, others put the descent to Hades amongst the youthful adventures of the hero and others state that towards the end of his life, Theseus decided to abdicate voluntarily. According to these last two versions of the myth, the hero died on Skyros at the hands of the king Lykomedes, who pushed him from a rock. In 475 BC, Kimon brought back the bones of Theseus from Skyros to Athens and placed them in a heroon (the Theseion) which had been built in his honour.

Athenian men and women dance the geranos, as they embark on their ship at Delos.
(Volute krater, c. 570 BC. Florence 4209.)

THESEUS AND HERAKLES

The myths concerning Herakles and Theseus have many points in common, but also some important differences. One basic point of similarity between the two heroes is their divine origin, which gives them superhuman powers; they successfully deal with many different kinds of monstrous beings, such as the Lernaian Hydra and the Minotaur or the Cretan bull and the bull of Marathon. They could be described as benefactors, since they rid the ancient world of various elements that threatened the social order and prosperity.

Despite this, however, their motives, and their characters, were radically different. Herakles was by nature wilder and had a quicker temper; he killed his own family and committed several pointless murders, of which even the Delphic oracle refused to purify him (such as when he exterminated the family of Eurytos because of his amorous desire for Iole). Herakles wandered the entire world to carry out his labours and in the end did not settle in any one place. Indeed, three different areas of Greece lay claim to him: the Argolid, which was his place of origin, Boeotia, where he was born, and Aetolia, the home of his wife, Deianeira. According to the myth, his troubled life was due to the grudge borne by Hera against his mother, Alkmene. This was the account given by the myth-makers to delineate the personality of a hero who travelled from one end of the world to the other, and whose feats were known throughout the length and breadth of Greece.

In contrast, Theseus, once he had grown to manhood, was directly connected with only one city, Athens, in which he lived and over which he ruled. Furthermore, he carried out his labours of his own free will and not as a result of compulsory service to another. He seems to be more pacific by nature, since he does not cause conflict (compare the seizure of the Delphic tripod by Herakles), but for the most part takes only defensive action to protect his city and his rights. Theseus is not only a mighty warrior, but also concerns himself with the political affairs of his country (the *Synoikia*) and was the model of the king who worked indefatigably for the security and prosperity of his land.

Ultimately, however, Herakles

Herakles attacks Geras, the personification of old age.
(Amphora, c. 470 BC British Museum E 290.)

defeats death, whereas Theseus dies, meeting an inglorious death for a hero like himself. The view has been advanced that the labours of Herakles symbolise the struggle against death; this interpretation seems probably enough, when one considers that the hero descended to the Underworld and returned to earth with the fearful Kerberos, while Theseus only managed to return from his journey there with the aid of Herakles. Herakles' indefatiga-ble struggle for life is suggested by a scene on an amphora in the British Museum, in which the hero is using his club to pursue Geras, the personification of old age. Through his adventures and the torment that marked his life on earth, Herakles secured a place in Mount Olympos, and immortality and eternal youth, while Theseus died like any mortal, despite being honoured as a hero.

THE ACHAIAN
EXPEDITION TO TROY

The events of the Trojan War
are sung in epic poetry, which was a major source
of inspiration both for artists and for the writers
of ancient tragedy.

THE CAUSES OF THE WAR

According to the epic tradition, the cause of the war was the protest by Gaia at the remorseless increase in the human population; the goddess suffered greatly from the weight of her burden, and complained to Zeus. The father of the gods, noting the need to reduce the number of people on the earth, caused the war. The expedition against Troy, like many other long bloody conflicts was, according to Hesiod, the reason for the extermination of the race of heroes. The immediate cause of the war was the abduction of the 'fair Helen' by Paris. The son of the king of Troy visited the palace of Menelaos at Sparta, where he was welcomed with appropriate honours; his purpose, however, was to carry off the beautiful wife of the master of the house and take her to his homeland, in order to make her his own wife. How did this story begin, however? What force impelled Paris to violate

Memnon, with the support of a Trojan,
fights a duel with Achilles
for the body of the dead Antilochos.
(Detail from the east frieze of the Treasury
of the Siphnians at Delphi, c. 530 BC.)

the institutions of marriage and hospitality and ignore the terrible consequences that such an act of impiety might incur?

It all began at the wedding of Peleus and Thetis. Thetis was one of the daughters of Nereus, and had enchanted both Zeus and Poseidon with her beauty; a major conflict would have broken out between the two gods had not Themis, the goddess of Justice, come between them, and warned them that, if Thetis coupled with a god, she was destined to produce a son who would surpass his father and overthrow the existing balance in the world, which had been consolidated after so many struggles. The gods immediately saw reason and decided to marry Thetis to Peleus, a brave young man who ruled on Mount Pelion, where he had been sent by his father Aiakos, the king of Aegina. It was decided that Peleus would have to capture the Nereid in order to demonstrate that he was worthy of marrying a goddess. The hero called upon all his powers, for Thetis was indomitable and always managed to escape her opponents by changing form. One night at full moon,

when the Nereid was dancing with her sisters on the shore, Peleus suddenly appeared before her and held her tightly in his arms; the girl began to change form, now into a snake, now a dragon and now a lion, but Peleus did not let her out of his arms for a moment until Thetis became exhausted and surrendered to him.

The marriage of a goddess to a mortal was a major event, and all the gods honoured the imposing ceremony with their presence, offering gifts and prayers to the newly-weds.

Although no deity should have been missing from such an important event, Eris, the goddess of strife, had not been invited for obvious reasons. She naturally became aware of the festivities and decided to take her revenge for the insult offered her by causing a dispute which would have deadly consequences. She appeared at the wedding feast and offered a golden apple for the most beautiful goddess; her challenge was taken up by Aphrodite, Athena and Hera, who began to argue with each other about who was the most beautiful. Zeus intervened to

**Peleus attempts to seize Thetis, who transforms herself into a serpent to escape.
(Epinetron, 425-420 BC. Athens, National Archaeological Museum 1629.)**

put an end to the dispute and appointed Paris-Alexander as judge, ordering Hermes to take the three goddesses to him. Paris's father was Priam, the youngest son of Laomedon, and the only one who survived after Herakles laid siege to Troy. Priam had restored his father's kingdom and ruled together with his wife, Hekabe, and their children Hektor, Kassandra, Paris, Troilos, Polyxene and Deiphobos. The first signs of the impending disaster came when Hekabe was pregnant with Paris and dreamed that she had given birth to a torch that set fire to Troy and consumed it. As soon as their son was born, the two terrified parents gave him to a shepherd with orders to kill him, but the shepherd took pity on him and brought him up. Paris grew up into a handsome, intrepid young man, and was therefore given the name Alexander. He lived in the mountains of Troy grazing

**The procession of gods
at the wedding of Peleus and Thetis.
(Volute krater, c. 570 BC, Florence 4209.)**

Hermes takes Athena, Hera and Aphrodite to Paris,
who is playing the lyre as the grazes his flocks.
(Kylix, c. 490-480 BC. Berlin,Staatliche Museen F 2291.)

his herds, but later fate drew him to his real father, who recognised him.

Hermes took the three goddesses to the grazing grounds of Troy to meet Paris, but as soon as he found himself in their majestic presence he was so terrified that he ran to hide. Hermes reassured him however and revealed Zeus's orders to him. The goddesses approached him and tried to tempt him, not only with their beauty, but also with their gifts: Athena promised him strength and invincibility, Hera the kingdom of Asia and Europe, and Aphrodite the most beautiful woman in the world. When Paris gazed upon the goddess of love, he was unable to resist her allure and yielded to temptation.

His decision took him to Sparta, to the palace of Menelaos, the hus-

NEMESIS   TYCHE   PEITHO   HELEN   APHRODITE

band of the 'fair Helen'. In order to satisfy the desire planted in his heart by Aphrodite, the hero had to win the most beautiful woman in the world and make her his wife.

It was the will of the gods that Paris should leave Sparta with Helen, for this act of impiety would lead to war between the Achaians and the Trojans and therefore satisfy Gaia's demands.

This myth was embellished by the ancient tragedians, who added that the underlying cause of the war was the terrible curse that lay upon the house of Atreus, the father of Agamemnon and Menelaos. Their misfortunes began with Tantalos, who ruled over a large area of Asia Minor, probably the region of Lydia. Tantalos was very popular with the gods and often dined with them on Mount Olympos; on one occasion, however, he decided to test the wisdom of the immortals and gave a dinner in their honour, at which he offered them his son, Pelops, to eat. The gods at once realised the deceit and were angered at the arrogance of their favourite. They brought the unfortunate Pelops back to life, by sewing the pieces of him together, and condemned his father to eternal torment by hunger and thirst in the midst of a lake with an abundance of water and rich vegetation.

When Pelops reached marriageable age, he learned that Oinomaos, the king of Pisa in Elis, had announced that any youth who succeeded in defeating him in a chariot race would marry his daughter. The king adored his daughter, Hippodameia, however, and therefore never allowed anyone to beat him; he obliged the suitors to take the bride-to-be with them in their chariot during the contest, which acted as a handicap and allowed Oinomaos always to win. Pelops learned of Oinomaos's trick and decided to pay him back

Aphrodite and her followers attempt to persuade the 'fair Helen' to follow Paris to Troy. (Amphoriskos, c. 430-420 BC. Berlin Staatliche Museen 30036.)

HIMEROS   PARIS   HEIMARMENE

in the same coin. By his persuasive words and promises, he won over the king's faithful charioteer, Myrtilos, who loosened the lynch-pin in one of the wheels of Oinomaos's chariot, causing his death. When Myrtilos later asked for his reward, Pelops killed him so that there would be no witness to his deceit; before he died, however, the charioteer cursed him.

Pelops married Hippodameia and became king in the Peloponnese; his kingdom was blessed by the gods, because Hermes gave him the sacred sceptre of authority which had originally been presented to Zeus by Hephaistos. From their marriage were born two sons, Atreus and Thyestes, and a daughter, Nikippe; Pelops also had a third, illegitimate son, Chrysippos, on whom he doted. This relationship aroused the fatal jealousy of his wife, who conspired with her two sons to kill Chrysippos. The curse of Myrtilos had brought disaster to the kingdom of Pelops who, crushed by the death of his beloved son, cursed his own family: to escape their father's wrath, Atreus and Thyestes fled to their sister, who had married king Sthenelos and lived at Mycenae.

The curse of Pelops was to sow discord between the two brothers when, years later, they aspired to the throne of Mycenae. Sthenelos was originally succeeded by his son, Eurystheus, but when he was killed by the descendants of Herakles, the throne had to be occupied by one of the Pelopidai. Although Atreus, as first-born son, had inherited the sacred sceptre of authority from his father, Thyestes managed to cheat his brother and rule himself. Zeus could not permit so great an injustice, however, and intervened to restore order. When Atreus became king, he learned that his brother had attempted to cheat him, and indeed to attain his end had an affair with his wife, Aerope. Blinded with rage, Atreus killed Thyestes' children after which he invited Thyestes to the palace on the pretext of a reconciliation and served him his own children for dinner. When Thyestes became aware of this terrible crime, he cursed his brother and his descendants and left Mycenae; in his despair he turned to the oracle to ask how he could be avenged, and he was told that the son he would bear by his own daughter would destroy the family of Atreus.

And indeed, the incestuous relationship between Thyestes and his daughter Pelopia produced Aigisthos, who was abandoned by his mother in the mountains, out of shame at her impious act. There he was found by Atreus who, unaware of his identity, took him in and brought him up as his own child. Eventually Thyestes reappeared at Mycenae, and the king sent Aigisthos to kill him, but his father recognised him as his son and conspired with him to kill Atreus. With the aid of Aigisthos, who had been born to destroy the Atreidai, Thyestes succeeded in seizing the sceptre of power from his brother and ascending to the throne of Mycenae, while Atreus's children, Agamemnon and Menelaos, fled to Sparta.

The kingdom of Sparta was ruled by Tyndareus with his wife Leda and their children the Dioskouroi (Kastor and Polydeukes), Helen and Klytaimnestra. Tradition has it that the Dioskouroi and Helen were the children of Zeus, who had approached the enchanting Leda in the form of a swan; this accounts for the courage of the two heroes and the incomparable beauty of their sister. Tyndareus affectionately welcomed the children of Atreus to his palace and treated them like a father. When they grew up he married Agamemnon to Klytaimnestra and helped him to return to Mycenae to claim the throne of his father, while to Menelaos he gave his beautiful daughter Helen, and appointed him his successor to the throne of Sparta.

The brothers were rulers of the most important kingdoms in the Peloponnese, at Mycenae and Sparta. Agamemnon and Klytaimnestra had three children, Iphigeneia, Orestes and Elektra, while Menelaos and Helen had an only daughter, Hermione.

Their happiness could not last long, however, since it was overshadowed by the heavy curses of their ancestors – Myrtilos, Pelops and Thyestes. And when the goddess Aphrodite sent Paris to Sparta, their lives took a dramatic turn.

After the end of the chariot race, Pelops has taken Hippodameia in his chariot and leaves Elis. In the background are depicted two courting doves, a symbolical reference to the future marriage of the young couple. (Amphora, c. 420-410 BC. Arezzo, Archaeological Museum 1460.)

THE PREPARATIONS FOR THE EXPEDITION

As we have just seen, the 'fair Helen' went with her young suitor to Troy, either through force or through persuasion. The abduction of his wife was a great insult to Menelaos, who immediately began preparations for war in order to defend the honour of his family. In this he was greatly assisted by the oath given by the suitors of Helen to her father, Tyndareus. Helen's beauty was famous throughout the whole of Greece, and when she reached marriageable age, there were many who aspired to her hand. Tyndareus wanted to be sure that the other suitors would accept his decision without protest, and made them swear an oath that they would all jointly defend the honour of his daughter if anyone should ever insult her. Since the strongest kings of Greece were bound by this oath, Menelaos quickly assembled the army he needed.

The Greek forces finally gathered at Aulis, from where they were to embark on their long voyage. It was then, however, that the first piece of ill-fortune occurred: as Agamemnon was hunting in the sacred forest of Artemis he killed one of her deer. The goddess was incensed at the hero's presumption, and caused the winds to drop, so that it would be impossible for the ships to put to sea. The prophet Kalchas, who was accompanying the army, predicted that the only way to propitiate the goddess would be to sacrifice the first-born daughter of the king, Iphi-

geneia. Again it was Odysseus who undertook to go to Mycenae. By telling Klytaimnestra that Iphigeneia was to become the wife of Achilles, he managed to bring her away with him. Meanwhile, in Aulis, the preparations had been made for the sacrifice; when Agamemnon raised his sword to kill his child, however, Artemis felt sorry for the girl and took her away from the altar, replacing her with a deer; the goddess took Iphigeneia to Tauris (on the Crimean peninsula) where she became a priestess in her sanctuary there.

When the Greeks had sacrificed the deer, believing it to be Agamemnon's daughter, favourable winds began to blow and the ships set off on their voyage; one of their ports of call was Delos, where they paid honour to Apollo.

Finally, after various adventures, the Greeks arrived at the port of Troy and encamped outside the walls of the city.

Agamemnon raises his knife
to sacrifice Iphigeneia,
while Artemis replaces
the girl with a deer.
(South Italian krater,
c. 370-350 BC.
British Museum F 159.)

THE TENTH YEAR OF THE SIEGE AND THE END OF THE EXPEDITION

For nine long years the Greek army had been besieging Troy and the city had not fallen. The events of the war had thrown the entire Greek world into turmoil, and indeed the gods themselves, who closely followed the outcome of the struggle from Mount Olympos, were divided into two camps: Hera, Athena, Poseidon, Hermes, and Hephaistos supported the Greeks, while Ares, Apollo, Artemis, Leto and Aphrodite were on the side of the Trojans (see p. 45).

Many heroes distinguished themselves for their courage in the clashes that took place over this time. Outstanding amongst them was Achilles, who captured Troilos (one of Priam's sons) at a spring outside the wall of Troy and then sacrificed him to Apollo. He also excelled in all the battles, leading his army courageously both in attacks on the walls of Troy and in raids on neighbouring areas to gain supplies. Achilles had won some valuable booty from these raids, including two beautiful girls Breseis and Chryseis. Breseis was the daughter of Breseus and lived with her husband Mynetos at Lyrnessos, from where Achilles abducted her to make her his mistress; Chryseis, who was priestess of Apollo on the island of Chryse, was in Thebes in Asia Minor (on the coast of Adramyttion) when Achilles invaded the city

and, entranced by her beauty, abducted her to give her to Agamemnon.

The myth took a dramatic turn when Chryses, the father of Chryseis, who was also in service in the sanctuary of Apollo, came to Troy intending to offer ransom to purchase the freedom of his daughter. Agamemnon at first refused to be parted from his beautiful mistress, not realising that his decision would incur the anger of Apollo. And indeed the god punished his impiety by spreading a pestilence and great destruction in the Greek camp. Agamemnon was then obliged to give way, but on condition that Achilles would give him Breseis. A delegation was immediately appointed to bring the girl from

'The games for Patroklos'.
A chariot race in honour of the dead Patroklos. Athletic games were traditionally organised in the honour of a hero who had fallen on the battlefield. (Fragment of a dinos, c. 580-570 BC. Athens, National Archaeological Museum 15499.)

Breseis returns to Achilles after the death of Patroklos.

Achilles' tent to the tent of the king of Mycenae. The Greek leaders had to find a compromise solution to temper the wrath of the gods as quickly as possible, otherwise their army was in danger of being wiped out. This decision, however, slighted Achilles, who in protest withdrew from the battle, together with his warriors.

Although the rest of the forces continued their attacks for some time without Achilles' assistance, the Trojans came very close to the Greek camp at one stage and threatened to capture it. Alarmed, Patroklos, asked his close friend, Achilles, to lend him his army so that he could enter the battle and save the situation. Recognising the seriousness of the turn of events,

Achilles agreed on condition that Patroklos would merely hold off the Trojans and would not go on to the attack; he then gave his friend his powerful weapons and ordered the Myrmidons to fight at his side.

When Patroklos entered the battle wearing Achilles' armour, everyone believed that it was the hero himself, who had decided to swallow his wrath in view of the critical situation. The Trojans were thrown into panic at the sight of the fearsome warrior and turned to flight. In his enthusiasm at his success, Patroklos ignored the terms of the agreement he had made with his friend, and started an attack to capture the city. Apollo, however, was watching the bat-

The spring at which Achilles set an ambush to capture Troilos,
because, according to an oracle, if the young son of Priam lived beyond
his twentieth year the city of Troy would never fall into enemy hands.
(Volute Krater, c. 570 BC. Florence 4209.)

tle from the walls of Troy, supporting the inhabitants of city, and
checked Patroklos's impetus by
wounding him with one of his arrows. By the time the hero had realised what had happened and had
regrouped his men, Hektor had fatally wounded him. A fierce battle
followed to prevent the body of Patroklos falling into the hands of the
enemy and the Greeks finally managed, with great difficulty, to bring
the dead man back to their camp.

Achilles' grief at the loss of his
beloved fellow warrior and friend
was unbearable. His comrades
tried in vain to alleviate his suffering and Agamemnon immediately
returned Breseis to him without
demanding any recompense. The
hero could think of nothing but revenge, however, and, overwhelmed
by his sorrow, asked his mother to

Achilles drags the body of Hektor
behind his chariot.
(Lekythos, c. 510 BC. Delos Museum 546.)

procure some new armour for him. Thetis knew that if her son entered battle again he would be killed, but Achilles was obdurate and ignored her warnings. the Nereid had no other choice but to help him, and went to Hephaistos's workshop and asked him to make new weapons within a single day (see p. 50). Thetis was moved by this and took the weapons to Achilles, who at once assembled his army and rushed into battle to exact his revenge on the man who had caused him such great grief. Hektor soon realised that he would not return alive from this clash, but his conscience and character would not allow him to submit. He bravely fought a duel with

Ajax lifts the body of the dead Achilles on to his shoulders to take it from the battlefield.
(Volute krater, c. 570 BC Florence 4209.)

**Memnon, with the support of a Trojan, fights a duel with Achilles.
(Detail from the east frieze of the Treasury of theSiphnians at Delphi,
c. 530 BC. Delphi Museum.)**

Achilles and died a hero's death.

Over the following days Achilles continued to fight with the same strength. His most famous contest was with Memnon, the king of the Ethiopians and ally of the Trojans. Memnon was also the son of a goddess; he had been born by Eos, who brought the dawn, and his father was Tithonos, Priam's brother. Despite this, Achilles managed to defeat him and immediately began an attack on the walls of Troy. Apollo, however, ever vigilant for the safety of the city, directed Paris's arrows to the vulnerable heel of Achilles, causing the death of the hero. Telamonian Ajax, from Salamis, at once lifted Achilles' body on to his shoulders, while the other Greeks fought around him, opening a path for him to return to the camp.

The death of Achilles caused great grief amongst the Achaians, who organised in his honour the athletic competitions that were usually held in the memory of heroes, and then buried him together with his beloved friend Patroklos. The elaborate weapons of Achilles, to which both Odysseus and Telamonian Ajax laid claim, were given to Odysseus after a vote; the decision was influenced by the goddess Athena, who knew that the wily king of Ithake would make a major contribution to the success of the expedition. Ajax felt himself slighted because his great strength had been disparaged, and put an end to his own life.

Despite these unpleasant events, the Greek leaders summoned an assembly with the aim of arriving at a strategic design to capture Troy. Their decisions were significantly influenced by the prophetic words spoken by the seer Kalchas, who predicted that if their aim was to be achieved, the following had to happen: Achilles' son, Neoptolemos, had to be summoned to the battle; the weapons of Herakles had to be used, which were in the possession of Philoktetetes (see p. 82), whom they had abandoned injured on the island of Lemnos before they even reached Troy; and the Palladion had to be stolen. The Palladion was the sacred wooden statue of Athena which was said to have fallen from heaven (*diïpetes*) and to have been found by Troas, the founder of Troy and his father Laomedon. Troas had set it up in his city and paid it great honour, believing that it was a heaven-sent sign of his power; consequently, if anyone was to steal the Palladion, Troy would lose the symbol of its strength and would be destroyed.

Diomedes carries the Palladion to the Greek camp from the temple of Athena in Troy.
(Kylix, c. 400-390 BC. Oxford 1931.39.)

These were the prophecies made by Kalchas and Odysseus set out to carry them out.

Athena implanted another design in Odysseus's mind, which supplemented his successful capture of the Palladion; this, of course, was the device of the Wooden Horse.

The hero got the camp carpenter to make a huge wooden horse, big enough to hold a military unit in its hollow belly. In this way, the Greeks would enter Troy and capture it. But how were they to persuade the Trojans to take the Wooden Horse into their city? Odysseus's plan was indeed very wily: he first chose the warriors who would accompany him in the belly of the horse, and then the rest of the Greeks struck camp, embarked on their ships and, led by Agamemnon, sailed out of the harbour of Troy and anchored off the island of Tenedos. Those left behind took the Wooden Horse to the walls of Troy, leaving in the camp only Sinon, who was to put the plan into practice.

Sinon pretended that he was being hunted, and hid in some vegetation, intending the enemy to see him. The Trojans, who were bewildered by the sight of the Wooden Horse, at once captured him intending to get as much information as they could out of him. Sinon was not loth to talk, and began by saying that his fellow countrymen had left, going on to reveal to them the whole story: Athena had been angered by the theft of the Palladion and had sent great disasters to punish the Greeks; in the confusion, Kalchas had prophesied that the only way to propitiate the goddess was to take the Palladion to Greece and to offer the Wooden Horse in her temple in Troy. Sinon went on to explain

The Greek soldiers inside the Wooden Horse.
(Amphora with relief decoration, c. 670 BC. Mykonos Museum 2240.)

his own position: he said that because of his differences with Odysseus, he had become alienated from his fellow warriors. When the ships were preparing to depart, Kalchas announced that they had to sacrifice Sinon to secure the favour of the gods and a favourable wind, as they had done at Aulis with Iphigeneia. In the end, he had managed to escape from the altar and had thus remained behind at Troy.

Sinon's story was believed by the Trojans, who brought the Wooden Horse inside their city and began to celebrate the end of the war. The only ones to realise the misfortune, were Laokoon and Aeneas. Laokoon attempted to warn his fellow countrymen, but was not believed; while he was sacrificing to Poseidon, two serpents emerged from the sea and strangled him together with one of his sons, and the Trojans interpreted his death as divine punishment because he had not believed in the sanctity of the Wooden Horse.

The capture of Troy was well planned. When the Trojans were completely disorganised as a result of their celebrations and the wine they had drunk, Sinon ascended to a high point of the city and sent a fire signal to Agamemnon instructing him to return with the ships. Then Odysseus's men emerged from the Wooden Horse, opened the gates of the city, and began a merciless slaughter. The tragic nature of the battle is well caught in a kylix in the Louvre Museum, on which Neoptolemos, the son of

Achilles, kills Priam, despite the fact that the latter has taken refuge as a suppliant at the altar of Zeus, and hurls Hektor's son, the young Astyanax, from the walls of the city so as to eliminate the last descendant of the royal family. All around them warriors fight hand-to-hand. An equally horrifying act of sacrilege was perpetrated by Lokrian Ajax from Central Greece, who raped Priam's daughter, Kassandra, even though she had sought protection as a suppliant at the statue of Athena. Athena was shocked at his sacrilegious act, and punished the impious hero by sinking him and his ship as he was returning to his home.

After a ten-year siege, Troy had finally fallen and Menelaos's honour had been restored. The Greeks assembled at their ships, taking much booty with them, including the Trojan women, and prepared to set off back to their homelands. However, they were punished severely for the barbarous and impious acts that they had committed when they entered the city of Troy. The Achaians lost their ships as a result of natural disasters and storms caused by the gods, and many of them met with tragic deaths. Even those who did finally manage to return, had to wander for many years before they did so, and even in their homelands great misfortunes awaited them.

The fall of Troy.
(Kylix, c. 490 BC Louvre G 152.)

THE END OF THE ATREIDAI

Agamemnon, delighted with his triumph, took his army and fleet and set off back to his own land. The most precious piece of booty he had won was Kassandra; she was the daughter of Priam, to whom Apollo had given the power of prophecy; when she refused to sleep with him, however, the god cursed her that her predictions would never be believed. Kassandra knew well the tragic end that was waiting both for her and for Agamemnon at Mycenae, but since no-one would believe her prophetic words, she silently followed her fate.

Orestes has taken refuge at Delphi to escape the Furies.
One of the Furies can be seen behind the Delphic tripod threatening him and holding snakes in her hands. The hero turns in despair to Athena, who seems ready to help him, while Apollo avoids his eye and looks at one of the Furies.
(South Italian bell krater, c. 350-340 BC. British Museum.)

**Orestes murders Aigisthos in the presence of Elektra and Klytaimnestra.
(Drawing from a stamnos, c. 470 BC. Berlin, Staatliche Museen F 2184.)**

During the ten years of war, there had been tragic developments in the palace of Agamemnon, for the triple curse that weighed upon the family had not yet been accomplished. Aigisthos, the son of Thyestes, who had been born to take vengeance on the Atreidai for the sacrilegious act of their father, had succeeded in winning Klytaimnestra to his side. When she heard of the death of Iphigeneia, Klytaimnestra conceived a hatred for her husband and in her despair she sought consolation in the arms of Aigisthos; she sent her son, Orestes, to be brought up in the palace of Strophios, the king of Phokis, and kept only Elektra with her.

This was the situation in Agamemnon's palace, when the king arrived unsuspecting at Mycenae. The presence of Kassandra was one more reason for Klytaimnestra to take revenge on her husband. At first she welcomed him with great honours; she had prepared a luxurious bath supposedly for him to relax, but as soon as Agamemnon was unarmed and vulnerable, Aigisthos appeared and killed him. Kassandra shared the same fate.

Aigisthos succeeded Agamemnon and ruled with Klytaimnestra at Argos and Mycenae for eight years. When Orestes grew up, he consulted the oracle of Apollo and decided to return to native country to avenge the death of his father. Orestes came to Mycenae accompanied by his faithful friend, Pylades, the son of the king of Phokis, with whom he had grown up. He first met his sister, Elektra, who told him all that had happened and encouraged him to kill the adulterers. On a stamnos in Berlin the hero, with the support of Elektra, pierces Aigisthos's breast with his sword, while Klytaimnestra threatens him with an axe; she will soon share the fate of her second husband, however.

Despite his motives and intentions, Orestes was nevertheless a matricide, and the Furies could not overlook such an impious crime. The terrible goddesses of the conscience began to pursue the hero relentlessly. Orestes, sought refuge at the Delphic oracle in the hope that Apollo would help him. This episode is depicted on a column krater in the Louvre Museum, where a winged Fury pursues Orestes, while he takes refuge at Apollo's altar; the god holds a laurel branch in his hand and turns his gaze on the Fury and restrains her impetus with a gentle gesture of his hand. Orestes was in the end acquitted by the court of the Areopagos in Athens, and the deities of the conscience ceased to persecute him.

In another version of the myth, Orestes meets his lost sister, Iphigeneia. According to an oracle, Orestes would only be completely purified and free of the persecution of the Furies, if he brought the cult statue (*xoanon*) of Artemis from Tauris to Greece. In the sanctuary of Artemis in Tauris, however, where Iphigeneia was priestess, strangers were sacrificed at the goddess's altar in her honour, and this was the fate awaiting Orestes when he arrived at the sanctuary together with his comrade, Pylades. The two heroes, however, chanced to meet with Iphigeneia, who spoke to them full of nostalgia for her family and asked them what had been happening in her absence. Their discussion led to the recognition of the brother and sister and, together with Pylades, they took the sacred *xoanon* of Artemis and returned to their homeland.

Orestes ultimately succeeded to the throne of his father at Mycenae, and moreover added Sparta to his kingdom by taking the daughter of Menelaos as his wife; by his marriage to Hermione he had a son, Teisamenos, who later succeeded him.

During the reign of Teisamenos, the descendants of Herakles returned to Mycenae. As we have already seen, the Delphic oracle had predicted that the third generation of Herakleidai would rule in the hero's place of origin, and the interval of time envisaged had now elapsed.

The Herakleidai dethroned Teisamenos and made themselves kings of the most important cities of the Peloponnese. The cycle of the family of Pelops had been come to an end, as, too, had the period when the kingdom of Mycenae was at its height.

THE TROJAN WAR.
FROM MYTH TO HISTORY

The events that disturbed the troubled heroic period are preserved in many myths that were handed down in different versions, and which cannot be encapsulated in a brief, concise account.

The basic core of the Trojan myth is formed on the basis of the Epic Cycle, a series of epic poems with a cyclical narrative, which opens with the causes of the war and ends with the return of the heroes to their homeland; the events leading to the Trojan War were recounted in the *Kypria Epe*; Homer's *Iliad* described the tenth year of the siege of Troy and the wrath of Achilles; the *Aithiopis* is an account of Achilles' duel with Memnon, who was king of the Ethiopians and ally of the Trojans; the tragic fall of Troy is narrated in the *Iliou Persis;* the *Nostoi* is an account of the adventures of the Greeks as they return to their homeland; and Homer's *Odyssey* narrates the ten years' wandering of the wily Odysseus before his return to Ithake. The Epic Cycle contains several references to the troubled history of the family of Pelops, Atreus and Agamemnon, but more information on this subject can be derived from the ancient tragedies.

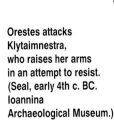

Orestes attacks Klytaimnestra, who raises her arms in an attempt to resist. (Seal, early 4th c. BC. Ioannina Archaeological Museum.)

The tragedians retained the basic core of the myth as formulated in epic poetry, but embellished it with dramatic elements more appropriate to the spirit of ancient tragedy, thus creating a wide range of different versions. The three plays of Aeschylus's trilogy, the *Oresteia,* which was highly popular, were based on a single theme: the events that took place at Mycenae after Agamemnon's return from Troy. The first tragedy is called *Agamemnon,* and describes the king's arrival at Mycenae and his tragic death, the second is called *Choephoroi* and deals with Orestes' matricide and its fearful consequences for the hero, while in the third, the *Eumenides,* Orestes is freed from the persecution of the Furies. The meeting between Orestes and his sister at Mycenae is described by Sophocles and Euripides in two tragedies entitled *Elektra,* and Euripides also deals with Orestes' adventures in his tragedy named after him. Euripides was also inspired by the myth of Iphigeneia and composed his tragedy *Iphigeneia in Aulis* which deals with the sacrifice of the girl to Artemis, and another entitled *Iphigeneia in Tauris,* which describes Orestes' journey to Tauris and his meeting with his lost sister.

As we can see, the myth relating to the rule of Pelops and his descendants in the Peloponnese was very popular in ancient poetry; this circumstance is probably due to its direct connection with the so-called Mycenaean civilisation, which was centred on the kingdom of Mycenae. The outstanding finds brought to light by the excavations of Heinrich Schliemann have shown that between the 14th and 11th century BC there was an important civilisation at Mycenae that enjoyed great prestige and influence; the decline of this civilisation in the 11th century BC is connected with the destruction of the palace at Mycenae.

Many theories have been advanced as to the causes of this destruction, most of them connecting it with the presence of the Dorians in this area. According to one view, the Dorians moved south from Boeotia or Thessaly and invaded the Peloponnese at the beginning of the so-called Dark Age (11th c. BC). Other scholars, however, do not believe that the descent of the Dorians was a sudden catastrophic invasion, and assert that they gradually penetrated the Peloponnese and were peacefully assimilated into the local population; according to this latter theory, the Dorians came to power by exploiting the decline of the Mycenaean palaces, which was the result either of economic collapse or destructive natural events such as earthquakes.

According to the myth, the Atreidai were expelled from the

Peloponnese when the Herakleidai invaded. After the death of his father Herakles, Hyllos attempted to wrest the throne of Mycenae from Eurystheus; despite killing his opponent, however, he did not succeed in winning power because the oracle at Delphi had predicted that it would only be the third generation of Herakles' descendants who would successfully invade the Peloponnese. In the meantime, power was assumed by the Atreidai, in the following sequence: Atreus, Thyestes, Agamemnon, Aigisthos, Orestes and Teisamenos, who ruled over Mycenae, Argos and Tiryns, the two last also adding Sparta. The downfall of these rulers was their personal passion and thirst for power, and the Trojan war was added to their internecine conflicts with tragic consequences. When the third generation of the Herakleidai returned to the Peloponnese, it had no difficulty in driving from power the last of the family of Atreus: it was in any case the will of the gods.

It is difficult not to associate the mythical invasion of the Herakleidai with the collapse of the powerful kingdom of Mycenae, which is confirmed by archaeological evidence. Unfortunately, however, we can only guess at the causes of this destruction. We do not know what historical events inspired the epic poets to recount

Gold funeral mask, the so-called 'mask of Agamemnon'.
(From a tomb in Grave Circle A at Mycenae. Middle of the 16th c. BC. Athens, National Archaeological Museum 624.)

the heroic expedition against Troy; the powerful kingdoms of Mycenaean times probably organised military expeditions to distant lands in order to increase their power both territorially and economically. All that we can be certain of is that in the 11th century BC the palace at Mycenae was destroyed and Mycenaean civilisation went into decline; it may be that the Trojan War, or other similar ambitious enterprises, did not yield the expected benefits, and together with a variety of internal conflicts led to the economic collapse of the palace at Mycenaean; or perhaps the gods had concluded that the descendants of the hero Herakles had wandered long enough and the time had come for them to return to their homeland.

ODYSSEUS

Odysseus, the famous king of Ithake, was son of Laertes and Antikleia. His wife was Penelope, by whom he had a son, Telemachos. In the *Iliad*, Homer describes Odysseus as one of the most charismatic of the Achaian leaders, distinguished by his courage and cunning, who makes a major contribution to the positive result of the expedition. The hero's return to Ithake, and his wanderings and adventures over a period of ten long years, are narrated by the poet in the epic *Odyssey*.

When Troy had finally fallen, and the 'fair Helen' had returned with Menelaos to Sparta, the victors set off home to their homelands. Odysseus gathered together his companions, put the spoils he had won on his ships, and set off for Ithake. The first port of call on the journey was the island of the Kikones, which he captured; he respected the priest of Apollo, however, and in return the latter gave him valuable vases and utensils and twelve flasks of wine. A storm over the next days cast him up in the land of the Lotus-eaters,

The blinding of Polyphemos.
(Fragment of a krater, c. 660 BC. Argos, Archaeological Museum.)

who cultivated the lotus flower; Odysseus rejected their hospitality, however, when he realised that anyone who ate the fruit of this plant forgot his homeland.

The wind then brought him to the land of the Kyklopes, where his many adventures began. According to Homer's account, the Kyklopes had only one eye in the middle of their forehead, were wild and lived a pastoral life, dwelling in caves and tending their flocks. Odysseus and his comrades cast anchor off the land of the Kyklopes and went ashore to investigate, but encountered the inhospitable man-eating Kyklops Polyphemos, son of Poseidon. He trapped them in his cave, which he sealed by placing an enormous rock at the entrance, and then seized two of the men and swallowed them. Odysseus realised that they would only escape through some trick, and put a cunning plan into practice. First he offered the Kyklops wine to drink, and when he was drunk and fell asleep, he heated the trunk of an olive tree in the fire and thrust it powerfully into his opponent's only eye. The following morning, the Kyklops, enraged at what had happened to him, stood outside his cave and felt the backs of his animals as they came out of the cave to go to

Odysseus escapes from the cave of the Kyklops bound under the belly of a sheep. (Bronze figurine, c. 575-525 BC. Delphi Museum.)

their grazing ground, intending to catch the men who had blinded him. Odysseus and his comrades, however, had tied themselves underneath the bellies of the sheep, and managed to escape safely to their ships. When Polyphemos realised that the strangers had eluded him, he laid a curse on their leader, that he should lose all his companions, should wander for many years, and when he finally arrived home, would find great misfortune. Polyphemos called upon Poseidon to fulfil his curses and the god, out of sympathy for his offspring, compelled Odysseus to wander the sea for ten years.

When Odysseus came to Aiolia, he was entertained by Aiolos, the lord of the winds; to help Odysseus, Aiolos gave him a flask in which he had shut up all the winds except the one that would take him back to Ithake. During the voyage, however, Odysseus fell asleep and his companions, out of curiosity, opened the flask and set free the winds, who took them back to Aiolia. From there they had to continue their journey unaided, because Aiolos refused to oppose the will of Poseidon for a second time.

The next adventure took place in the land of the Laistrygonians. The inhabitants of this country were enormous, very strong and naturally aggressive. They attacked Odysseus's companions, whom they decimated. The hero managed to escape and save himself together with just a few of them. They next anchored at Aiaia, the island of the goddess Kirke, and sent twenty men to reconnoitre. All of them except Eurylochos, went to the palace of the goddess, who was at first friendly and hospitable; as soon as she had gained their confidence, however, she raised a magic wand and turned them all into swine. When Eurylochos returned in panic to the ship and told the others what had happened, Odysseus decided to get to the bottom of the mystery himself. At this point the gods managed to escape Poseidon's watchful eye for a short time and help the hero. Hermes left Olympos and met Odysseus to give him a plant called *moly*, which would protect him from Kirke's spells. The goddess tried to turn him into a pig, but soon

realised that it was useless and in the end, enchanted by his power, she invited him to sleep with her. Before he accepted, however, Odysseus made her swear that she would not harm him and that she would release the spell on his comrades. Odysseus stayed on Kirke's island for a whole year, and shared her bed, but it was always his aim to return to Ithake. The goddess, respecting his wishes, urged him first to go to the Underworld to seek the advice of the prophet Teiresias, and she gave him directions for this difficult and dangerous journey. Odysseus headed north and, following the stream of Ocean, came to the river Acheron and the entrance to the dark kingdom of Hades. There he dug a trench and sacrificed a black ram and a black ewe in honour of Pluto and Persephone. As the blood flowed from the sacrificial victims, thirsty souls gathered around. The first to approach was the soul of Elpenor, an unfortunate companion of Odysseus who had been killed by an accident on the island of Kirke and had remained unburied. He now came to ask for burial and Odysseus promised him that as soon as he returned he would carry out his wishes. When Teiresias appeared, he first slaked his thirst with the blood of the sacrifice and then advised the hero not to allow his comrades to touch the flocks of Helios when they came to Thrinakia (in Sicily). He also warned him that other misfortunes would be awaiting him in Ithake and that he would have to propitiate Poseidon in the following way: he should take an oar on his shoulder and set out to find the country whose inhabitants did not know what the sea and ships were; when he got there he should stick the oar in the ground and sacrifice a boar, a ram and a bull in honour of the god; then when he returned to Ithake he should offer sacrifices to the twelve gods. Finally, the wise prophet, having predicted that

death would come to the hero from the sea, departed. After this Odysseus immediately permitted all the other souls to drink the sacrificial blood, and met with many that he knew and loved.

Homer gives a particularly moving account of his meeting with his mother, Antikleia, who had died of her grief and worry as she waited for him to return. Odysseus also met many of the heroes, including Achilles and Patroklos, Agamemnon, who told him about his own tragic death, and Theseus and Peirithoos, and he saw Minos and Rhadamanthys judging the souls and Sisyphos and Tantalos

**Odysseus, bound to the mast of his ship,
resists the seductive song of the Sirens.
(Stamnos, c. 475-460 BC. British Museum E 440.)**

suffering their eternal punishments.

When he returned to the island of Kirke, he attended to Elpenor's burial and prepared to depart. The goddess warned him that he would pass by the Sirens, who had women's heads and the bodies of birds, and who enchanted passers-by with their intoxicating singing, making them forget their homelands to stay with them. When Odysseus's ship neared the island of the Sirens, the hero ordered his companions to tie him to the mast and block up their ears with wax. Odysseus was enchanted by the sweet voices of the Sirens, but could not escape from his bonds.

Next the hero had to steer a course between two rocks which were inhabited by two menacing monsters. On one side lived Skylla, a terrible beast with six heads, who snatched anyone that dared to come near and tore them apart, while on the other was Charybdis, who swallowed the sea and then vomited it out creating sudden storms and whirlpools. Odysseus managed to overcome this obstacle, though he lost another six of his companions.

The next port of call was Thrinakia where, heeding the advice of Teiresias, he forbade anyone to touch the flocks of Helios. However, by mischance, bad weather broke out and they were obliged to stay on the island for a month, so that the supplies given to them

Skylla on the waves,
(Bronze sheet, late 4th. c. BC. Athens, National Archeological Museum.)

by Kirke ran out. At one point, when Odysseus was away, Eurylochos was driven by his hunger to persuade the rest to kill some of the animals and then propitiate the god by sacrifices and honours. Helios, however, was slighted and punished them severely: before they could sail away he overturned their ship, sparing only the life of Odysseus. The hero wandered the sea clutching to the ruins of the ship until, after nine days, he came to Ogygia, the island of Kalypso.

Odysseus spent about five years with the beautiful Nymph, who promised him that if he would stay forever with her, she would grant him immortality and eternal youth. He, however, desperately wanted to return to his homeland, and wept as he gazed out to sea and thought of Ithake. When Athena saw her protege in this state, she took pity on him and, taking advantage of Poseidon's absence, asked Zeus for help. It was at once decided that Hermes should be sent to Kalypso to tell her that it was the order of the gods that she should set Odysseus free, and Athena herself went to Ithake to urge Telemachos to visit Pylos and Sparta in search of news of his father.

Kalypso obeyed the orders of the gods and bade farewell to Odysseus, first helping him to make a raft and supplying him with the necessary provisions. The adventures of the hero were not yet over, however. As Poseidon was returning to Mount Olympos, he noticed the raft and in his anger caused a fearful storm. Odysseus fought with the waves unaided for two days, until he came to the shore of the island of the Phaiacians.

The Phaiacians dwelt on Scheria and were a highly privileged people: their trees produced fruit at all seasons of the year, and their ships were magic, because they could sail without the aid of captains. Scheria was ruled by Alkinoos and Arete, his wife, who had four sons and a daughter called Nausikaa. On the day that the storm cast up Odysseus on the island, the girl and her friends had gone down to the beach to wash. There she met the hero, who was naked and in distress, took pity on him, and gave him clean clothes, before taking him to her father's palace. Alkinoos readily entertained the stranger, and when he discovered who he was, honoured him with valuable presents and promised that would help him to return to his own land.

And Odysseus indeed came back to Ithake on one of the magic ships of the Phaiacians. The hero was welcomed to the home he had yearned for by Athena, who told him all that had happened

Penelope sits in sorrow next to her loom, and her son, Telemachos stands before her.
(Drawing from a skyphos, c. 440 BC. Chiusi, Museo Civico 1831.)

during his absence. During the ten years of his wanderings, all trace of him had been lost and many thought that he was dead. The suitors of his wife Penelope, had established themselves in the palace. One hundred and eight men were eating and drinking daily at the expense of his estate, waiting for Penelope to decide which one she would choose to become her husband. She, however, secretly hoped that Odysseus was still alive, and delayed answering. Meanwhile, the suitors had lost their patience and, to put Penelope in an even more difficult position, were plotting to kill her son, Telemachos, when he returned from Sparta, where he had gone to seek news of his father.

These were the difficulties encountered by Odysseus when he returned to Ithake, but he overcame them with the aid of Athena. First of all, the goddess told him to dress as a beggar so that his enemies would not recognise him, and brought Telemachos to him, to protect him from the suitors' conspiracy. When father and son recognised each other, they agreed to work together to restore order to their land.

Odysseus appeared at the palace dressed as a beggar and no-one recognised him apart from his aged dog, Argos, who died as soon as he saw his master. The suitors treated the poor stranger with great contempt, and he suffered their jeers and attacks. That evening, having advised his son to remove the spears from the walls of the banquet room, he visited Penelope, though he chose not to reveal himself to her yet. He told her that he had heard that her husband was on the island of the Phaiacians, where he had gone to acquire more wealth before returning finally to his home. Although she found it difficult to believe that Odysseus would return to her, Penelope took care of the stranger and asked Eurykleia to wash his feet. Eurykleia, the aged nurse of the hero, recognised him from a mark on his foot, but promised him not to reveal his secret.

Next day, events moved rapidly. Penelope showed the suitors Odysseus's bow and told them that she would marry anyone who could bend it and fire an arrow through twelve axes. One by one the suitors attempted to bend the bow and string an arrow on it, but no-one had the strength. Then Odysseus, still dressed as a beggar, humbly sought permission to try. Everyone laughed at him, but in the end gave permission. Great was their surprise, when the hero succeeded in bending the bow and shooting the arrow through the axes. Odysseus immediately revealed his identity and the suitors tried to escape in panic; they were trapped, however, because Telemachos had closed all the exits, and Odysseus used his bow to take revenge on all those who for ten long years had taken advantage of his palace and his estate.

Only after he had discharged his duty did the hero present himself to his wife in his real form. Penelope tested him to confirm that he was telling the truth, and then welcomed her husband with great emotion. The aged Laertes, the father of Odysseus was equally overjoyed when he saw his son. Odysseus told them all about his adventures, and lived with them happily. He did not fail to propitiate Poseidon, following Teiresias's advice, and died on Ithake many years later, precisely as the prophet had predicted: when Telegonos, his son by Kirke, arrived at the island in his ships, he clashed with the locals and killed their king, not knowing who he was.

Odysseus meets his wife, Penelope.
(Relief from Milos,
c. 475-450 BC. Louvre CA 105.)

OTHER MYTHICAL FIGURES
THE ARGONAUT EXPEDITION

Kretheus, the son of Aiolos, the lord of the winds, had his palace at Iolkos in Thessaly. The family of Kretheus was divided after his death, because his second-born son, Pelias, usurped the throne from the first-born, Aison, the father of Jason.

When Aison lost his kingdom, he gave Jason to the Centaur Cheiron to protect him from his enemies. Jason grew up secure in the mountains of Pelion, exercising his mind and body under the leadership of the wise Centaur. When the first two decades of his life had been completed, he decided to return to Iolkos to claim the kingdom that had been usurped by his father's brother.

Jason's arrival at Iolkos was from the very first an event of ill omen for Pelias. The youth entered the city wearing only one sandal, because he had lost the other on his journey. Pelias was terrified at this apparently insignificant detail, because he remembered the oracle that had warned him that he would lose his life at the hands of a 'one-sandalled man'. In order to keep his throne, and indeed his very life, Pelias decided to assign an impossible task to Jason: to claim his father's throne, the hero had to bring the golden fleece from the sacred grove of Ares in Kolchis, the country ruled by Aietes. First he had to succeed in crossing the ocean separating Thessaly from Kolchis and then seize the golden fleece from the fearsome serpent that guarded it.

It was a long journey and a very difficult mission, and the hero therefore had to secure a

Orpheus and other musicians sing to accompany the journey of the Argonauts. (Metope from the "monopteral" temple at Delphi, 590-580 BC. Delphi Museum.)

The sons of Boreas chase off the Harpies to rescue Phineus from his torment. (Gold and ivory relief, c. 570 BC. Delphi Museum.)

stout boat and able companions. Fate began to smile on Jason from the moment that Athena took his part. The goddess asked the famous craftsman Argo to make a swift ship for fifty oarsmen, and she herself oversaw the work. In a very short time the beautiful ship Argo, as it was called after its maker, was ready and Jason had to find a crew for it. The fifty young men that accompanied him were called Argonauts and their mission the Argonaut expedition. As in Herakles' expedition against the Amazons and the hunt for the Kalydonian boar, the most famous heroes from all over Greece took part in the Argonaut expedition: Herakles from Boeotia, Theseus from Athens, Amphiaraos from Argos, the Dioskouroi from Sparta, Meleager from Kalydon, Peleus from Thessaly, Kalais and Zetes, the sons of Boreas, the god of the north wind, and many others. Orpheus from Thrace kept time for the oarsmen with his enchanting music and calmed the sea with his singing: in the scene on a metope at Delphi, Orpheus with his lyre, together with another musician and two horsemen (possibly the Dioskouroi) are boarding the Argo.

As they crossed the Aegean sea, the Argonauts stopped at various places and faced many dangers. In Thrace they encountered king Phineus, who had blinded his two sons, because he believed the lies told him by their stepmother. For this act of injustice Phineus had been harshly punished by Zeus. The god condemned him to lose his sight and sent the Harpies, winged female deities, to torture him by stealing his food. Kalais and Zetes freed Phineus from his torture by driving off the Harpies; in return he gave the Argonauts instructions on how they could safely reach their destination, and sent favourable winds for their voyage. The episode is depicted on a gold and ivory plaque in the Delphi Museum. The two Harpies run of with Phineus's food, pursued by the two sons of Boreas; of the figure of the king, only part of the arm is preserved, which can be seen above the table.

Following the advice of Phineus, the Argonauts came to Kolchis. Their adventures had not come to an end, however.

Aietes did not agree to give them the golden fleece, but to avoid a conflict, set certain conditions. He agreed to meet their demand if Jason succeeded in ploughing a field using two divine fire-breathing bulls; after this he had to sow the teeth of a serpent and kill the Giants who would spring from them. The hero began to despair, but the gods once again offered him their support by firing arrows of love at Aietes' daughter, Medea, who knew the secrets of magic. The young girl, blinded by her love for Jason, decided to use her cunning and potions to help him. Having given him her magic ointment to protect him from the breath of the bulls, she told him to throw a stone amongst the giants in order to make them kill each other.

A warrior departs on an exepedition. (Ivory plaque, c. 570 BC. Delphi Museum.)

When Jason had successfully completed this difficult labour, Aietes refused to keep his promise, and in order to retain possession of the golden fleece tried to burn the Argo. Nothing could stand in the way of the hero, however, who had the gods on his side. Medea led Jason to the grove of Ares and helped him to get the golden fleece by putting the serpent to sleep with one of her magic potions. After this she did not hesitate to kill one of her own brothers, in order to delay her father's soldiers and give the Argonauts the chance to get away from Kolchis. Medea followed Jason and his companions and helped them in many adventures on their return voyage. Jason valued the dedication of the young woman and made her his wife.

When the Argonauts returned in triumph to Iolkos, Pelias refused to keep his promise. The god's oracle, however, was fated to prove true. To punish Pelias, Medea gave his daughters a magic potion and persuaded them that they would be able to make their father young again if they cut him to pieces and boiled him in it. The women followed the witch's instructions, and killed Pelias with their own hands.

Jason seizes the golden fleece. (Krater, early 4th c. BC. Naples, Museo Nazionale Archeologico 3248.)

Jason assigned rule at Iolkos to Pelias's son, Akastos, and himself set off with his family for Corinth, the kingdom inherited by Aietes from Helios. Medea, as a child of Aietes, was welcomed at Corinth and lived there happily for ten years with her husband and children. Their marriage, however, had a dramatic end; Jason fell in love with another woman and Medea, having taken vengeance on him by killing their children, was exiled from her country for the second time.

OEDIPUS AND THE THEBAN CYCLE

THE EARLY YEARS OF OEDIPUS' LIFE

Aeschylus told the dramatic story of Oedipus and his family in the trilogy formed by the tragedies *Laios*, *Oedipus*, and *Seven Against Thebes*, and the satyr play *Sphinx*. Only the third of these survives, but the plot of the others may be restored on the basis of other tragedies inspired by the same myth.

The story begins when Laios succeeded his father Labdakos,

Oedipus meets the Sphinx before the elders of Thebes.
(Pelike, c.460 BC. Vienna, Kunst Historisches Museum IV 3728.)

the son of Polydoros, to the throne of Thebes. The young king, and his wife Iokaste ruled happily over the glorious land founded by their great-grandfather, Kadmos. The years passed and because the couple had no children, they decided to consult the Delphic oracle. The oracle warned them that Thebes would be preserved only if they remained childless; otherwise it was ordained that the father would be killed by the hand of his son. Ignoring the prophetic words of Apollo, Iokaste became pregnant and brought a male child into the world. In their panic, the two parents attempted to cheat destiny: they ordered a faithful servant to abandon the new-born child on Mount Kithairon. The king even bound the young boy's legs together with chains around his ankle, to prevent him escaping. The servant, however, took pity on the baby and saved his life by giving him to a Corinthian shepherd he met on the mountain. The shepherd took the child back to his own land and delivered him to the king and queen of Corinth, Polybos and Merope, who were childless and received the child joyfully, calling him Oedipus, because his feet were swollen from the chains.

Oedipus was brought up as a prince in Corinth with the prospect of inheriting the throne of his father, without, of course, being aware of his true identity. The misfortunes began when someone accused him of not being the real son of the king. Distressed, Oedipus set out for the Delphic oracle in order to learn the truth. The Pythia, however, did not give a straight answer to the hero's question, but simply told him that it was ordained that he would kill his father and marry his mother. Shaken by the words of the oracle, Oedipus decided never to return to Corinth and began to wander from place to place. His travels gradually led him to the fateful meeting with his real father. In one of the narrow passes in Phokis, Oedipus's path crossed with that of Laios, who was travelling to Delphi to ask the oracle what had been the fate of the child he had abandoned on Mount Kithairon. The proud youth refused to give way to allow the king to pass, the two men clashed, and Oedipus killed Laios; the first part of the oracle

had been fulfilled. The unhappy youth continued his wanderings unsuspecting, while his dead father's attendants returned to Thebes with the bad news.

Kreon, the brother of queen Iokaste, was appointed successor to Laios and ruled the land together with the venerable elders.

The statue of the Sphinx which was dedicated by the Naxians in the sanctuary of Apollo at Delphi. (c. 570-560 BC. Delphi Museum.)

THE RIDDLE OF THE SPHINX

AT THIS TIME the diabolical Sphinx, a terrible monster with a woman's head and the body of a winged lion, appeared in Thebes and proclaimed that she would stop wreaking havoc in the land and destroying its inhabitants only if someone could solve the following riddle: 'What being may have two feet, four feet, or three feet, is the only one of all the beings that move on earth, in the air, and in the sea, that can change its form, and moves more slowly when it has most feet'. The Sphinx asked this riddle of anyone who went near her, and killed those who gave the wrong answer. In his despair, Kreon proclaimed throughout the whole of Greece, that anyone who succeeded in ridding Thebes of this suffering would become king of the land and would marry Iokaste. This proclamation brought Oedipus back to his birthplace. When the Sphinx encountered Oedipus she asked the riddle. The hero gave the correct answer, that the riddle referred to man, and in her rage, the Sphinx jumped from the rocks of the acropolis of Thebes and was killed. Thebes had been saved, and the 'saviour' married the queen, unaware of the tragic nature of his deeds.

THE REIGN OF OEDIPUS

OEDIPUS AND IOKASTE ruled at Thebes for several years and had four children: Eteokles,

Corinthian aryballos. 7th c. BC (Delphi Museum.)

Polyneikes, Ismene, and Antigone. Circumstances, however, led the king to realise his real identity (Sophocles, *Oedipus Tyrannus*). The cause was a drought that broke out at Thebes causing the death of many of its citizens. Oedipus, anxious for the fate of his country, sent Kreon to Delphi to ask how they could be rid of this scourge, and the god advised them to purify themselves of the pollution of the murder of Laios by driving the murderer from the city. The words of the oracle shocked Oedipus, who immediately proclaimed, with promises and imprecations, that he was determined to do everything he could to find the murderer, unaware, of course, that he himself was responsible for Laios's death. He first summoned the prophet Teiresias and made him reveal the truth. When the prophet broke his silence and revealed the tragic events, the king refused to believe him.

As the shocking truth began to be revealed, Oedipus recalled his clash in the past in Phokis, and his fears were confirmed when one of Laios's servants, the only one who had survived the conflict, recognised the king. His testimony was irrefutable, because he was the same servant who had taken the new-born child to abandon it on Mount Kithairon.

The royal couple met with a dra-

**Marble statue of a sphinx.
(540-530 BC. Acropolis Museum.)**

matic end. Iokaste hanged herself and Oedipus pierced his eyes with the pins that adorned the dress worn by his dead mother and wife. The hero blinded himself to conceal his unutterable shame in darkness.

The cloak of silence that had apparently protected Oedipus, was now lifted forever, marking the beginning of the end for the kingdom of Thebes. The blind king fled the land accompanied by his daughter, Antigone.

THE SEVEN AGAINST THEBES

THE THRONE OF OEDIPUS passed to his two sons, but they were unable to share power peacefully. After many fruitless negotiations, Eteokles became king and Polyneikes fled the city discontented, his only inheritance being the wedding presents of Harmonia, the wife of Kadmos.

The exiled brother went to Argos, arriving in he city the same night as Tydeus, the son of Oineus and Periboia, who had similarly been driven out of Kalydon to seek purification for the murder of one of his relatives. When the two youths met in the courtyard in front of Adrastos's palace, they quarrelled and came to blows. The king was awakened by their voices, but seeing them wrestling like wild animals, he realised that this was the fulfilment of a prophecy by the oracle that had told him to take the boar and the lion as his sons-in-law. He immediately intervened to separate the rivals, assuring them that they were both welcome in his palace. The relationship between Polyneikes and Tydeus developed into a strong friendship, and also kinship, for they married the two daughters of Adrastos, the former Argeia and the latter Deipyle. Adrastos offered his sons-in-law a life of ease and recognised them as his official heirs.

The two youths, however, had ambitions of returning to their own countries to claim the rights of which they had been deprived by exile. Adrastos, who effectively

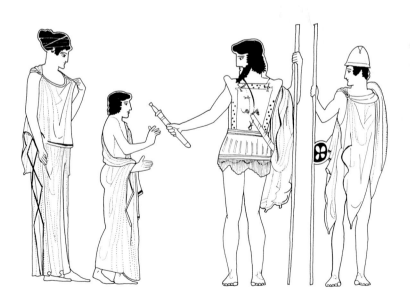

Amphiaraos entrusts his sword to his son, Alkmaion
(Drawing of a beu krater, c. 440 BC. Syracuse Museum 18421.)

had no other choice, agreed to help them by sending his forces first against Thebes and then against Kalydon. Before they set forth, they made one last attempt to settle the matter peacefully. Eteokles, however, refused to negotiate, even though Tydeus went to Thebes with peaceful intentions. Back in Argos, preparations began for the expedition, with the aim of assembling forces from neighbouring cities.

Adrastos at once turned to his brother-in-law, Amphiaraos. In the past these two men had quarrelled about affairs of state, but when they finally settled their differences, they sealed the reconciliation by a marriage between Amphiaraos and Eriphyle, Adrastos's sister, swearing an oath that in the future she would resolve any differences between them. Amphiaraos, who in addition to being a competent general was also a healer and a gifted prophet, foresaw the calamitous end of this expedition and refused to take part. Adrastos, however, knowing that he would make a very valuable contribution, refused to accept Amphiaraos's decision, and the two called upon Eriphyle to resolve their dispute. She had been bribed, however, by Polyneikes, with the necklace of Harmonia (the precious wedding present given by Aphrodite to her daughter) and therefore took her brother's side, betraying her husband. Adrastos could not foreswear his oath and therefore had to accept his wife's decision. Before setting forth, however, he handed his sword to his son, Alkmaion, ordering him to avenge his death by punishing his mother and undertaking an expedition against the Thebans.

When the preparations were completed, the army of the Argives and their allies set off for Thebes, but Polyneikes first went to Athens to find his father. After blinding himself, Oedipus had fled to Athens with Antigone (Sophocles, *Oedipus in Kolonos*). In the suburb of Kolonos, he had fallen as a suppliant at the altar of the Eumenides, and, having told his story to the venerable Athenian elders, had asked them to summon the ruler of the country, which at this time was Theseus, so that he could ask him to be allowed to die in Attica. While Oedipus was awaiting for Theseus, Ismene, his other daughter, came to Kolonos, to tell him about the war that had broken out between her brothers and to warn him that both of them would attempt to win him over, because according to the Delphic oracle, the battle would be won by the one that had Oedipus on his side. The first to arrive in Athens was Kreon, acting as the emissary of Eteokles, who tried to blackmail

Oedipus into cooperating by arresting his daughters. Theseus intervened, however, and drove him from the land. The next to arrive was Polyneikes, who attempted to win over his father by his moving words. Oedipus, however, was annoyed at the behaviour of his children and their thirst for power, and in his anger he uttered a curse that each would be killed by the hand of the other. Immediately after this the unfortunate king, after receiving a message from the gods in the form of a thunderbolt from Zeus, went off to meet Charon, who would take him to the Underworld. Theseus went ahead of the blind old man and promised him that he would offer help and protection to his daughters.

The clash between the Argives and the Thebans was to lead to the tragic end of Eteokles and Polyneikes, (Aeschylus, *Seven Against Thebes*). Eteokles was told about the arrival of the enemy while he was attempting to reassure the Theban women, who in panic had sought asylum at the altars of the gods. Each of the seven Argive generals had drawn up his forces in front of the seven gates in the walls of Thebes, in the following order: Tydeus, Kapaneus, Eteoklos, Hippomedon, Parthenopaios, Amphiaraos and Polyneikes. Eteokles gave his final orders to his army and decided to defend the seventh gate himself, fighting against his brother. The first step towards the fulfilment of their father's curse had been taken, and the battle ended in the retreat of the Argives, and with the two brothers killing each other.

This tragic event was not the end of the misfortunes of the family of Oedipus, however. Kreon, who came to power in Thebes once more, buried Eteokles with great honours, but forbade the burial of Polyneikes and refused to hand over the bodies of the seven generals to the Argives. This injustice and impiety towards the dead aroused a hostile reaction on the part of many. Foremost amongst them was Antigone, who declared categorically that she would not allow her brother to remain unburied.

Kreon decided to place a guard around Polyneikes's body, so that the dead man should remain exposed and be eaten by the animals, which caused the situation to deteriorate (Sophocles, *Antigone*). Incensed at this act of barbarism, Antigone attempted symbolically to throw a little earth on the abandoned body of her beloved brother, for which she was arrested, led to the king and finally punished by imprisonment. Kreon refused to revoke his order, even though he knew that as long as the established burial customs did not take place, the soul of the dead man would not find serenity, but was condemned to eternal torment. It was only when the prophet Teiresias warned him that an act of such great impiety directly endangered his life that he was obliged to allow Polyneikes to be buried. Kreon did not go unpunished, however. He first lost his son, Haimon, who committed suicide when he learned that Antigone, his fiance, had hanged herself in prison, and then his wife, Eurydike, who could not bear the pain of the death of her child.

Kreon's decision not to hand over the bodies of the seven generals to the Argives had equally dramatic consequences. The mothers of the dead men decided to seek the aid of Theseus, who was king of Athens at this time (Euripides, *Iketides*). Accompanied by Adrastos, the only general to survive the expedition, they came to Attica. The women fell as suppliants at the altar of the goddess

Amphiaraos heals a sick man.
(Votive relief, c. 400-370 AD. Athens, National Archaeological Museum 3369.)

Demeter at Eleusis, asking Aithra to persuade her son to help them. Theseus listened carefully to his mother, and then spoke respectfully of the dead and compassionately of their relatives, and agreed to satisfy the women's demand. To this end he led an expedition against Thebes. The Thebans, who were already weakened by the war, succumbed quickly to the Athenian forces and were obliged to hand over the bodies of the Argive generals. The bodies were taken to Eleusis, where they were buried with the appropriate honours by their wives and children.

The conflict was not yet at an end, however. Before departing for Thebes, Amphiaraos had given his son, Alkmaion, his sword, fore-

seeing that he himself would not return from the war. And indeed, as he was racing in his chariot to escape the enemy, the earth opened and swallowed him. This event was interpreted as a divine sign, and the first sanctuary of Amphiaraos was built on this spot: ever since then, Amphiaraos has been worshipped as a prophet and a healer-god.

THE EXPEDITION OF THE EPIGONI

ANOTHER EXPEDITION against Thebes was organised by Alkmaion, who had sworn to avenge his father's death, and Thersandros, the son of Polyneikes, who

wanted to lay claim to the throne of Thebes. The armies of the Epigoni assembled at Argos ten years after the first conflict. Their leaders were: Alkmaion, son of Amphiaraos, Thersandros, son of Polyneikes, Diomedes, son of Tydeus, Sthenelos, son of Kapaneus, Promachos, son of Parthenopaios, Medon, son of Eteoklos, and Polydoros, son of Hippomedon. The aged Adrastos offered useful advice and instructions to the young generals and sent his son, Aigialaeus with them.

Thebes was ruled by Laodamas, son of Eteokles, who undertook the defence of his country. When the Argive forces reached Boeotia, the Thebans began to attack, striking at the camp of their rivals.

The first to be killed was Aigialaeus, but the Epigoni swiftly regrouped their forces and then Alkmaion fatally wounded Laodamas. The Thebans retreated within their walls, panic-stricken at the death of their king. The Argives then attacked and were victorious. The kingdom of Kadmos had been completely destroyed — so comprehensively that it is not mentioned by Homer in the list of the Greek forces that took part in the expedition against Troy.

**The seven Argive generals prepare for the expedition against Thebes.
(Kylix, c. 490-480 BC. Louvre G 271).**

ASKLEPIOS

Asklepios was the son of Apollo and Koronis from Thessaly. Asklepios was a famous expert in and teacher of medicine; he had the gift of being able to heal all kinds of illnesses and to relieve men of their pain. His popularity, however, was also the cause of his death. The rumour that Asklepios was even able to raise the dead perturbed Zeus, who naturally did not wish men's belief in his own omnipotence to be shaken; the only solution was to put an end to Asklepios's life, and he therefore threw his thunderbolt and killed him.

After his death, Asklepios was honoured as a god. The most important of his sanctuaries was founded in Epidauros in the early 5th century BC, and thousands of believers from different parts of Greece flocked to it to be healed. The pilgrims first sacrificed to the god and took part in purification rituals, which prepared them physically and spiritually to enter the *enkoimeterion*, the sacred building where the god appeared to them in their dreams and told them the appropriate remedy for their complaint. Asklepios cured simpler illnesses while the sick person was asleep, but the more serious cases were assigned to his priests, who carried out the course of treatment prescribed by him.

Large numbers of votive reliefs have been discovered in the sanctuaries of Asklepios, offered in gratitude by the faithful towards their benefactor-god. The simplest of these depict only the specific part of body that was in need of therapy, and are in some ways reminiscent of modern *ex votos*.

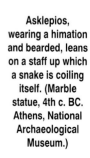

Asklepios, wearing a himation and bearded, leans on a staff up which a snake is coiling itself. (Marble statue, 4th c. BC. Athens, National Archaeological Museum.)

EUROPA
HER FOREBEARS AND DESCENDANTS

The continent of Europe is named after a princess who was born in Asia, but whose descent was from the Argolid. One of Europa's ancestors was Io, the daughter of Inachos, the king of Argos, who had been obliged to flee from her homeland because of the hatred of Hera.

Europa was the granddaughter of Libya, and daughter of Agenor and Telephassa, who ruled in Asia and had three more children: Kilix, Kadmos and Phoenix.

Agenor's family lived happily until Zeus fell in love with his beautiful daughter. The god turned himself into a bull and approached the girl when she was playing happily with her friends in the fields. The bull was so gentle that it did not frighten the girls and as it was amusing them with its games, Europa innocently sat on its back. The god did not miss this opportunity, but at once rose up into the air and went off taking Europa with him. Travelling over land and sea he brought her to Crete, which he had chosen as the place to couple with her; there Europa brought up their offspring, Minos and Rhadamanthys. The god also ensured that his beloved married the king of Crete, Asterios, so that his children should not grow up without a father.

**Zeus, transformed into a bull, carries Europa over the sea.
(Hydria, c. 370 BC.
British Museum E 231.)**

EPILOGUE

Myths played a very important role in Ancient Greek societies, because they were directly connected with their history and religion. Myths were woven to explain the natural phenomena that affected the daily lives of men, and also to narrate the historical events that marked the evolution of civilisation. Mythology was enriched throughout the whole of antiquity, with every place creating its own myths or producing variants of earlier ones, according to its own experience and needs.

Bronze theatre mask.
(4th c.BC. Athens, National Archaeological Museum.)

Through art and the written sources, we now know a great number of these myths, and are called upon to understand and interpret the role they played in the societies that created them. This is a difficult, never-ending task, which, as we have seen, produces conclusions that are mere hypotheses, since we can never fully enter into the ancient Greek mentality and tradition. Modern research is based mainly on analysis of the motifs of which the myths are composed, and seeks to interpret these in the light of their social and historical context. Many of the motifs in Greek mythology are repeated with different leading actors. Perhaps the most popular of them is the family conflict revolving around power. The first to become embroiled in this kind of clash were the earliest gods, who did not succeed each other peacefully: Kronos usurped the power of Ouranos, to be defeated in his turn by his son, Zeus. In the same way, Zeus prevented the birth of the son that would have been given him by Metis, when he learned that this child would surpass him strength. In the world of mortals, this kind of conflict arose mainly between brothers: we may recall by way of example Atreus and Thyestes, Aigyptos and Danaos, Proitos and Akrisios, and Eteokles and Polyneikes. These and other similar tales involving the deeds of men and heros, probably reflect human ambitions and dreams.

Only the gods are all-powerful, however, and can fulfil all their desires by using every possible means. They frequently transform themselves or transform their victims in order to achieve their ends: Zeus assumes the form of a bull to abduct Europa and Hera punishes

Io by turning her into a cow. The most precious gift they have to offer their favourites is immortality: it was for this purpose that Thetis baptised the new-born Achilles in the fire, as Demeter also did with the young Demophon. Fire is transformed into myth not only because it evoked awe in man, as indeed did the other elements of nature, but also because its contribution to the evolution of civilisation became apparent from a very early date. The possession of so important a tool and weapon naturally demanded an act of daring on the scale of that of Prometheus.

Many heroes were not merely the favourites of the gods but their offspring. The relationship between a god and a mortal woman, and vice versa, is a very common motif in Greek mythology. Herakles and Perseus, two of the sons of Zeus, and Theseus, the son of Poseidon, owe their superhuman strength to their divine descent. These heroes are called upon to face powerful foes, such as remorseless robbers and murderers, and also deadly beasts that threaten the social entity. They finally triumph thanks to their strength and the assistance of the gods, and tradition glorifies them by singing their adventures. The myths that tell of their feats form a model of courage and nobility, and their fight against various fantastic beings therefore symbolises man's struggle against unknown, and therefore terrifying, natural phenomena.

Every hero has his own story and his own personal labours, but there are also several cases in which many powerful men work together to confront an enemy or to carry out a mission. The choicest young men from the whole of Greece took part in the Argonaut expedition and the hunt for the Kalydonian boar, and when Herakles set out on his expedition against the Amazons and after that against Troy, he took with him warriors who were his equal, such as Theseus. And the most important kings of Greece took part in the famous Trojan War with their armies. All these myths reflect the adventures of the ancient Greeks in the Aegean and the Mediterranean in general, since Greece's geographical position acted as a stimulus to the evolution of shipping in antiquity, both for trade and for reasons of expansion.

The voyages and adventures of Greek sailors belonged to the world of myth and passed into eternity, like all the events that marked the troubled heroic age. It is true that the historical value of myths is debatable, but their contribution to the study of ancient Greek civilisation is invaluable. In the ancient world, men tell their stories through myths, and mythology is therefore an expression of their attempt to embellish and elevate their personal experience of life.

GENEALOGICAL TREE

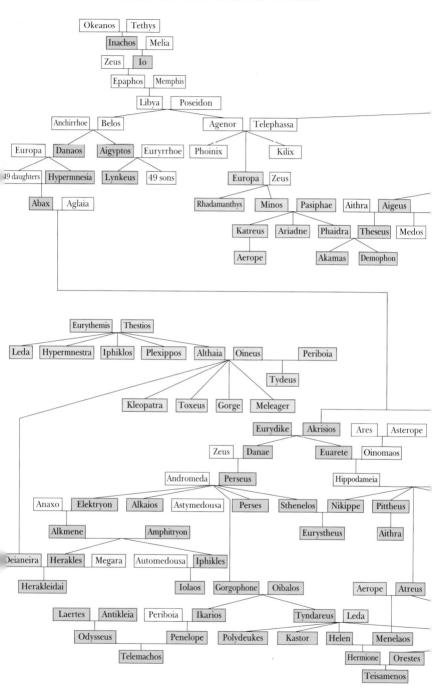

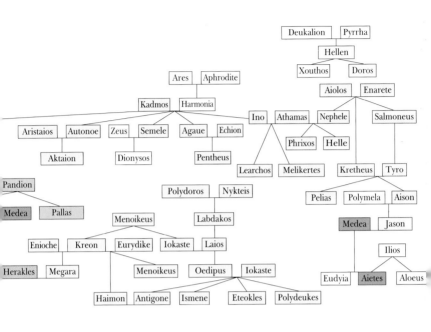

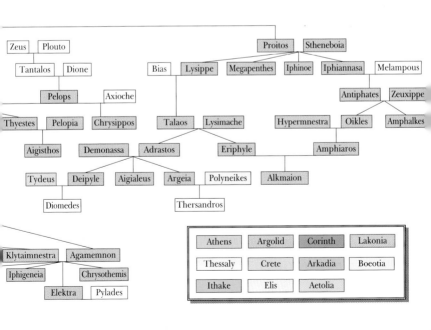

GENERAL BIBLIOGRAPHY

Armantrout, G. L., *The Seven Against Thebes in Greek Art* (1991).

Bell, R.E., *Dictionary of Classical Mythology* (1982).

Bieber, M., *The History of Greek and Roman Theatre* (1961).

Birchall, A. and Corbett, P.E., *Greek Gods and Heroes* (1974).

Boardman, J., *Athenian Black Figure Vases: A Handbook* (1974).

Boardman, J., *Athenian Red Figure Vases: A Handbook* (1975).

Boardman, J., *The Parthenon and its Sculptures* (1985).

Boardman, J., *Athenian Red Figure Vases, the Classical Period: A Handbook* (1989).

Bothmer, D. Von, *Amazons in Greek Art* (1957).

Bremmer, J. (εκδ.), «What is a Greek Myth?», *Interpretations of Greek Mythology* (1987).

Brommer, F., *Theseus: die Taten des griechischen Helden in der antiken Kunst und Literatur* (1982).

Odysseus: die Taten und Leiden des Helden in der antiken Kunst und Literatur (1983).

Heracles: The Twelve Labors of the Hero in Ancient Art and Literature (1985).

Brunel, P. (ed.), *Companion of Literary Myths, Heroes and Archetypes* (1992).

D. Buitron and B. Cohen etc., *The Odyssey and Ancient Art. An Epic in World and Image* (1992).

Burkert, W., *Greek Religion* (1985).

Burkert, W., *Structure and History in Greek Mythology and History* (1979).

Buxton, R., *Imaginary Greece. The Contents of Mythology* (1994).

Carpenter, T.H., *Art and Myth in Ancient Greece. A Handbook* (1991).

Chamay, J., *Mythologie grecque. La guerre de Troie* (1984).

Daltrop, G., *Die Kalydonische Jagd in der Antike* (1966).

Dowden, K., *The Uses of Greek Mythology* (1992).

Edmunds, L. (ed.), *Approaches to Greek Myth* (1990).

Graf, F., *Greek Mythology. An Introduction* (trans. Thomas Marier, 1993).

Grant, M. and Hazel, J., *Who's who in Classical Mythology* (1973).

Graves, R., *Greek Myths* (1955).

Grimal, P., *Dictionnaire de la mythologie grecque et romaine* (1991).

Kaempf-Dimitriadou, S., *Die Liebe der Götter in der attischen Kunst des 5. Jhs. v. Chr., Antike Kunst*. Elftes Beiheft (1979).

Κακριδής, Ι. Θ., κ.ά., *Ελληνική μυθολογία*, 1-5 (1986).

Κερένυϊ, Κ., *Η μυθολογία των Ελλήνων* (1974).

Kirk, G.S., *Myth. Its Meaning and Functions in Ancient Greek ad other Cultures* (1970).

Lesky, A., *A History of Greek Literature* (1966).

Lexicon Iconographicum Mythologiae Classicae (1981-).

Metzger, H., *Les représentations dans la céramique attique du IVe siècle* (1951).

Metzger, H., *Recherches sur l'imagerie athénienne* (1965).

Moret, J. M., *Oedipe, la sphinx et les Thébains. Essai de mythologie iconographique* (1984).

Neils, J., *The Youthful deeds of Theseus* (1987).

Nilsson, M., *History of Ancient Greek Religion* (1963).

Παπαχατζής, Ν.Δ., *Η θρησκεία στην αρχαία Ελλάδα* (1987).

Parke, H.W., *Festivals of the Athenians* (1977).

Schefold, K., *Myth and Legend in Early Greek Art* (1966).

Schefold, K, and Jung, F., *Die Göttersage in der klassischen und hellenistischen Kunst* (1981).

Schefold, K., *Die Urkönige, Perseus, Bellerophon, Herakles und Theseus in der klassischen und hellenistischen Kunst* (1988).

Schefold, K. and Jung, F., *Die Sagen von den Argonauten von Theben und Troia in der klassischen und Hellenistischen Kunst* (1989).

Simon, E., The Ancient Theatre (1982).

Simon, E., *Festivals of Attica* (1983).

Stewart, A., *Greek Sculpture. An Exploration* (1990).

Touchefeu-Meynier, O., *Thèmes odysséens dans l'art antique* (1968).

Trendall, A.D and Webster, T.B.L., *Illustrations of Greek Drama* (1971).

Vernant, J.P., and Vidal-Naquet, P., *Myth et Tragédie en Grèce ancienne*, vol. I, II (1972, 1986).

Vernant, J.P., *Myth and Society in Ancient Greece* (trans. 1983).

Vollkommer, R., *Herakles in the Art of Classical Greece* (1988).

Walker, J.H., *Theseus and Athens* (1995).

Woodford, S., *The Trojan War in Ancient Art* (1993).

DESIGN: **KOSTAS ADAM**

TEXT: **MARILENA KARABATEA**

TRANSLATION: **DAVID HARDY**

LAYOUT: **KRISTI KASASTOGIANNI**

DRAWINGS: **STELIOS DASKALAKIS**

PRODUCTION: **ADAM EDITIONS**

PERGAMOS EKTIPOTIKI EKDOTIKI